UPFRONT
PUBLISHIN

Wander

ISBN: 978-178456-687-6

Perfect Bound

First published 2019 by UPFRONT PUBLISHING
Peterborough, England.

An environmentally friendly book printed and bound in England
by www.printondemand-worldwide.com

Wander

We are all migrants. We emerge from our domicile in eternity. We participate in synchronicity. We must learn to "play" with imagination and reality, or they "play" with us.

Such is life.

www.billthompson.info

and

www.thesecularphilosopherbillthompson.uk

An extract from: An anthropological study, by Thomas Henry Huxley, 1886,

I conceive that the origin, the growth, the decline and the fall of those speculations respecting the existence, the powers, and the dispositions of beings analogous to men, but more or less devoid of corporeal qualities, which may be broadly incuded under the head of theology, are phenomena the study of which legitimately falls within the province of the anthropologist. And it is purely as a question of anthropology that I propose to treat of the development of theology in the following pages.

With theology as a code of dogmas which are to be believed, or at any rate repeated, under penalty of present or future punishment, or as a storehouse of anaesthetics for those who find the pains of life too hard to bear, I have nothing to do, and so far as it may be possible, I shall avoid the expression of any opinion as to the objective truth or falsehood of the systems of theological speculation of which I may find occasion to speak. From my present point of view, theology is regarded as a natural product of the operations of the human mind, under the conditions of its existence, just as any other branch of science or art.

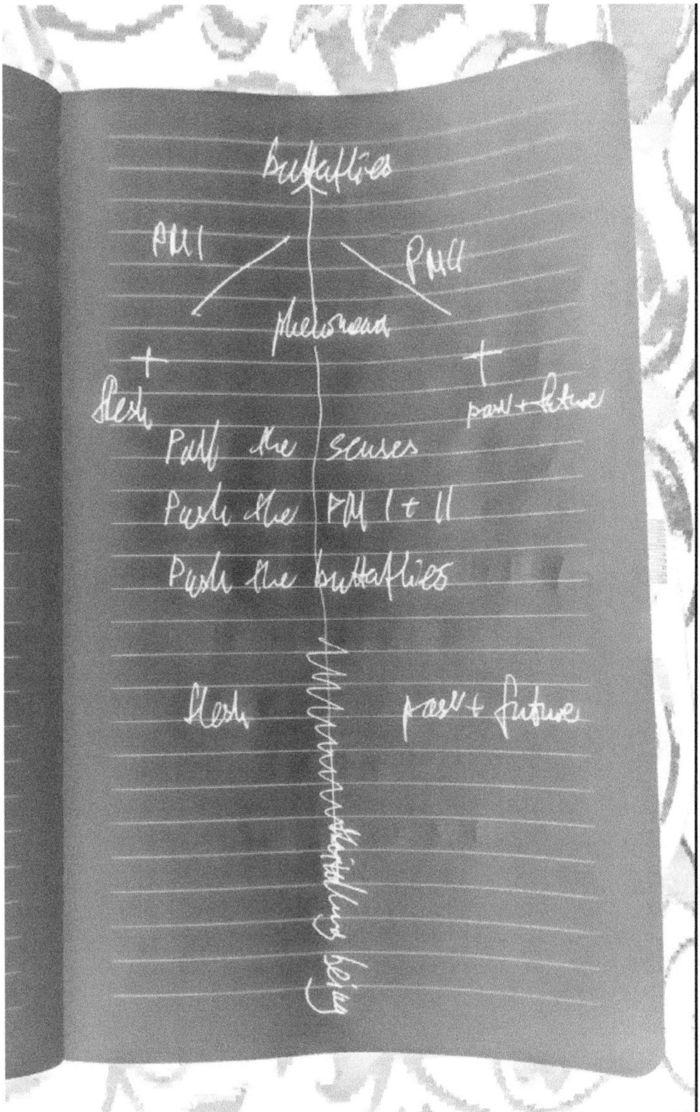
butterflies
PM I
PM II
phenomena
flesh
past + future
Pull the senses
Push the PM I + II
Push the butterflies
flesh
past + future

Leader

Interpretation relies upon imagination and feelings and appearances, then interpretation proceeeds according to beliefs about what appears

[which does so because of **PM1** & **PM2**

AND SYNCHRONICITY.

We "parole" the walk and domicile the "langue"

The interpretation leads to an understanding which is an halting of synchronicity, thus unreal, and yet substantive, thus we can, it seems, produce langue and

contribute **+** *and* **-** *with our paroles.* **But** *all "langues" are substantive in varying degrees and unreal in principle and thus all can turn into meaninglessness......*

Contents

Most individuals around the world now have heard of the term post modern. Other terms for this are post structural, post truth, and so on.

This book of mine does not deny truth. I try to explain the concept of post positivism, or creative realism as I call it, This requires us to alter the way we behave. A new common sense about existing together.

But the common sense we need is of the way we share the management of our interpretations of synchronicity and eternity. At present we all tend towards sharing what we call an understanding. This understanding is of ourselves, of others, of the world, of things, of the universe and so on.

But we each develop different understandings. What is needed is a shared management of the way we humans interpret our existence. It is our ability to interpret what is happening, synchronicity, that gives rise to understanding the differences between what is imagined and what is real. It is, for humanity, the naming of parts that allows us to share what we imagine and what we believe to be real.

The problem is that because we interpret individually we have to create nominal understandings, and those understandings have to relate to both common and individual interpretations. This is confusing unless individuals have already learnt to share a single nominal understanding so it seems. Thus we have developed cultures, languages, religions, social groups, institutions and so on and so forth.

The hard part of consciousness

It is only because more of us want to migrate from one culture to another peacefully that this book stands any chance of being read.

Up until now those "in charge of" cultures and institutions, for example, told "their flock" that we could live multiculturally. But maintaining cultures alongside other cultures makes for ghettos and despots rather than heterogeneous individuals existing together.

We need to change the way we share the management of interpretations because the specialisations we have resorted to in the division of daily practices have developed their own vernaculars in their own ghettos. This means that a gulf has developed between the quotidian, the everyday of specialists and the quotidian of most of the rest of us.

I believe we still need our ghettos and I explain why in this book. But I believe that the majority of us need more polymaths, persons who can share interpretation rather than understandings per se. So I offer this book as eight essays which taken as a whole explain my concept of a social pedagogy. A "spiritual res publica". A radical alternative to social engineering or social "cleansing", because the individual is the basic unit for socialisation.

Synchronicity is where each individual finds itself interpreting imagination and reality for itself. Our development as a species has been towards the realisation of our individuality, however as we have developed as snowflakes we have forgotten about snow.

My previous three books Smile, Voices and Play explain most of the technical details about interpretation by us as an organism. I ended my third book Play with an intellectual/materiality dichotomy. Since then I have developed this new synergy between imagination and reality that helps each of us to value our interpretations. The coherence of our individual understandings is however the thing that separates us. Thus if we wish to plan for some global common sense we must focus upon interpretation and the things that appear within synchronicity that we feel are important and meaningful for us, as individuals and as members of social groups of one sort and/or another, and ultimately as a species.

Thus by appreciating interpretation individually, using my acronym DEPTH, developmental existential phenomenal thermeneutics, we could learn to share the management of our behavour and thus deal with synchronicity as one species symbiotically. This seems to me to be the only way to arrive at a working symbiotic relationship with earth as snowflakes who recognise their domiciles as snow.

Essays In Order of Appearance:

Introduction

I taught "context" for 10-years at universities in the UK to 2010. My approach was to try and be a teacher-student. The concept of context was an appreciation of probable meaning. Being in context. Being meaningful and so on.

The point of this book is to encourage all of us to be teacher-students as a way of interpreting our possibly meaningful existence together.

The positivist enlightenment humanist claim that natural science can provide us with a description of reality and thus of truth and absolute meaning has been rejected by its own deeds. As we know from the many cultures, languages, religions, and schools of philosophy there are many outcomes of natural science all in conflict with each other. Indeed the work of archaeologists and sociologists up until the late 19th century brought about the current early 21st century belief in multiple "meanings", multiple contexts, multiculturalism, but this cannot remove conflicts between absolute faiths in absolute truths that are incommensurate with any other understanding.

The major influence in the development of all these is the concept of “the human”. Thus the expert in any culture is caught up in existential efforts to show causation and consequence for everything because of the need to be “wise”, an expert but of what exactly? The Human condition! And whereas races were thought to be, believed separate it now seems that we are all one race, the human race.

What seems to have gone unnoticed is that natural science is just one of many nominalised systems seeking to be wise about the human condition. It is just one, a large and currently impressive understanding, yet a culture none the less. Its teachers and learners have teamed up with “its” cultural “elites” to make a political economic wisdom. Each and every culture is however in what I call synchronicity. Thus the monoculture based on natural science, commonly called neo-liberalism presents itself in the experience of many of us around the world on a daily basis as a claim that its wisdom is outperforming all other understandings. Be that as it may, it is in conflict with them rather than in conversation with them.

What I hope to show, in these essays, is that this attempt at a competitive monoculture is not the best use we can make of our interpretive skills. One problem I have is that at the moment other cultures and religions and social groups treat the neo-liiberal culture as the enemy. The consequence is that there is emnity and violence rather than what I claim in this volume is a common interpretive skill we all have that can be shared and managed to our common advantage as a species so long as we learn to distinguish conversation as a part of developing wisdom. The biggest barrier to this seems to be the advantages of having faith in wisdom rather than a faith in our ability to find a common approach to the avoidance of suffering using hands and brains together. If we are all snowflakes, and all of humanity as one is snow, then we find a lot of snowwisdoms like snowmen, snowwomen and snowscapes all around the world. Thus although we are unique individually, we share the ability to appear as snow, with our own snowy landscapes as separate snowy landscapes.

The biological explanation of this seems to be the link between stabilty of the myth-reality or dream-truth relationship linked to some freedom in the imagination-reality relationship such that “flesh” [a metaphor of wisdom about the reality of what appears] and imagination are between them able to correlate behaviour to the level of risk and certainty an individual feels they can adhere to in order to reduce suffering as it may. In this sense life is a game but the wager can clearly demand high stakes or low stakes and has a basic condition that is real for all of us as to survival of the flesh and freedom of the imagination.

I have written about our common interpretive skills in my three earlier books Smile, Voices and Play. The technical and mechanical details of us as individuals having such skills as we have are laid out in them. The term I used is depTH in which the letters can be linked to developmental existential phenomenal Thermeneutics. The latter term is the “move” I make away from understandings of interpretation up to now, which others have generally taken to be analytical rather than interpretive. My argument is that even argument by rhetoric based on analysis of a “reality” based on language is patently risible. This is even more ludicrous now that we have biologists and cosmologists “telling us” we rely on a “chemical” electrodynamic milieu for survival as listed in our periodic table.

In order to develop from the fluidity of the chemical to the analytical however, we create the functionality of the that and how, the T&H of traditions that we adhere to when maintaining those traditions discussing “reality” pragmatically but manacled to language analytically rather than creatively, as required to make possible first conversation and then communication. Thus we create adherents to traditions that separate us from other traditions. This seems to be commensurate with what we find now about our settlement patterns around the globe. What we lack then is a better understanding of the dilemma of language as the choice between conversations, including “pointless” conversations, then communications and then wisdom.

About the Contents

in my first essay "**the voice as reason**" I discuss the importance of the verbal in describing the that and how of our experiences. I introduce the problem of "limbo" and the project.

In the second "**history as reason**" I discuss how diarising the that and how of experiences produces our concepts of both tradition and change out of limbo, but restricts us to the project.

In my third essay "**coherence**" I discuss how the project can quickly become a record of a tradition that we can adhere to. In adhering to the project mechanics we maintain tradition, but are condemned to choose wisdom rather than play.

In essay four ""**the idea of the eidetic**" I discuss how typically the discussions arising over our relationships to an adherence to tradition and any desire for change have been forced into rhetorical agonisms. The clarity of the argumentation depends on the ability of both sides to "see the argument" amongst what are actually at least two, usually many more separate "projects" set against a relatively coherent background of conversations wherever we go.

In essay five "**the model of social utopia**" I show how the eidetic condition of our rhetoric has produced what I feel is a mistaken impression in most traditions that each one of them can finalise their rhetorical agonisms and thus produce a utopia. This makes crossing cultures, disciplines and peer review conditions impossible in my opinion.

In essay six "**post-positivism**" I discuss what we must all do if we are to accept that the possibility of utopia is not only unlikely because of the fluidity of electrodynamics, but also because our attachment to the tradition and wisdom of a project makes us sclerotic.

In essay seven I discuss "**migration and morphosis**" as the way in which individuals seek to shift their here and now, that and how, to a tradition they like better than the one in which they feel they dislike or dislikes them. I explain why it is "normal" to experience an existential threat when this happens, yet it can pass.

In this final essay "**social pedagogies**" I discuss what seem to me better than older notions of social epistemology, and a lot better than older models of social engineering that use "empirical evidence" and "ethnic cleansing". This notion of social pedagogies is that what brings us to learning is the human condition itself as project-rich, [an alternative concept is "niche" rich, if only we can realise it]. We already deal with synergy individually, and the diversity of individual feelings is central to the feeling individuals have about settlement and survival. What I explain in these essays is that the settlement and survival is bonded to projects that overlap. Individuals can move between settlements because they are not so much virtual as chosen by choosing play or wisdom about projects, in effect.

The notion of simply giving up one settlement for another is the current model. This relatively new model, as social pedagogy, is the concept of socialisation as a symbiotic response to the planet, and to theories and practices relating to our locations on the planet that can be coherently adhered to by individuals thus becoming a suite of projects that are able to respond to both local and global projects using a combination of wisdom, play, and “authentic” participation. Futhermore I believe the trade off between nationalistic distinctions and the freedom to make coherent rejections of “the seduction of language” increases our ability to allow greater experimentations around basic survival, i.e. realities of the flesh and the imagination, per se, so that all settlements invite heterogeneous individualisms that add feel good factors when managed in the ways that we have become efficient at in terms of building our environments. By this I mean that heterogeneity could not in my opinion survive well if it was one project, or mass produced entirely. But we have arrived at the stage where the private/public boundaries need no longer require walls and already benefit from our abilities to construct them, in terms of “real” and imagined boundaries. A term I like for this concept is the spiritual res publica or spiritual public realm – a non vitalist pragmatic and even secular spiritualism!

The Voice as Reason

in this first essay “**the voice as reason**” I discuss the importance of the verbal in describing the that and how of our experiences. I introduce the problem of “limbo” and the project.

-

Whereas I am loath to claim that we are special I believe it is nonsensical [though it can be “fun”] to believe we are not human. Thus I claim that as humans our interest is human whether we like it or not. Individuals are free to detest the apparent fact of being born as human, just as some of us declare we detest what appears to us as the body we are born with [even though it changes all the time] and so on. Animals not blessed with a total language may make a noise about similar issues, but it isn’t at all clear what they are “noising about”. We on the other hand can make our gripes, and to be fair, compliments, crystal clear.

Individual humans are human, for various reasons many individuals seem to wish to be social, and all individuals are global. We wander the earth or may do so if not hindered or prevented from doing so.

There is a species symbiosis with the earth on which we are domiciled as a species. We settle in settlements of various sorts and sizes over much of the surface of globe, mostly the dry surfaces but in terms of living on boats, in boats and so on, then we settle on the water too. The concept of some of us being more human than others, more pragmatic, more romantic, more idealistic, more or perhaps less than others in some or all of these, is not uncommon. This has led to a tradition of common or garden exchanges of opinion on many issues and more or less at the drop of a hat. These opinions can become more shaped and fashioned according to the flow of conversations. If I call the conversations centripetally and centrifugally inclined then the latter opens up the conversation, the former shapes and fashions it towards some focus. That focus could be a repugnanace of some kind or an attractiveness, it depends. In this way, in the everday common run of conversations, we have the somewhat peculiar situation of a species that can converse about the that and how of their opinions for so long as they choose. This can all be done quite literally over a fence, or in a small room, or in an open field. The huge difference between us and other "things" that I would like to call "phenomena" is that they cannot do this at all it seems, as Bickerton [1926-2018] and others aver. My point is not that no other creatures can "communicate" but that they do not have this kind of verbal ability to converse about every single that and how, when where and why, in the universe. In this sense we use phenomena [things] to articulate every other phenomenon that we can think of as well as the phenomena we use in the articulation, the words we use in speaking. The vast majority of us do it every day and with anyone who is willing to do it with us, and we can even do it on our own as a soliloquie, talking to ourselves. The that and how happens and we can describe and imagine the that and how.

One of the quite recent approaches in theory related to the here and now of facts concerning the that and how of everything, is to consider "being" as within a tradition or culture as a participant. One who examined this concern was Heidegger [1889-1976] whose work was founded on a Lutheran [1483-1546] concept of faith, pistis, "belief in being". Most opinions seem to me to be based on this notion of believing in them, or hoping or supposing or expecting others will. This foundational basis was seemingly urged on from Heidegger's mentor Bultmann [1884-1976] if Jonas [1903-1993] is correct in his understanding of Heidegger as a fellow student at the time of his own studies. Another influence upon Heidegger was the work of Nietzsche [1844-1900]. The term existentialist is used to describe Nietzsche's interest in anxiety about meaning and meaninglessness. In my experience most individuals giving their opinions have very few anxieties of that sort. But if they did, and in most cases they should in my opinion, then Nietzsche has a point. Are all these opinions meaningful and do we care? Is the fact that opinions can be given a sign of truth, or rather a sign of some fear of an existential limbo?

The Heideggerian model of being is based upon the culture, but his concept of the bringing into being of culture is the concept of culture itself. The rules and axioms of a culture are considered to be inherent in the culture. The appearances of things, phenomena, within a culture were also important to Heidegger and the term phenomena was used to refer to appearances after the term used by Husserl [1859-1938]. These phenomena were considered to be internal to the organism, the human being, and Heidegger successfully related the internal phenomena to experiences of being in the world, i.e. existing. Describing existing would be a description of the that and how of it as an a-priori, an “already being”.

Heidegger also seems to have solved the issue of authenticity as to meaning within this culture, any culture so to speak, as meaningful within the knowledge of the culture, yet not supposing the culture had all the answers. Thus an authenticity of participation is this perhaps relaxed attitude to there being any absolute one to one relationship between the understanding of the culture and the outcomes that occur as a “member” or participant of this culture. Thus the individual came to know the culture but also, if accomplished as an existentialist knowingly or not, i.e. with anxieties about the reality of their belonging in and to and with that culture.

Individuals can understand that “meaning” was always there but had to be worked at, considered as fragile we might say. In general conversations this seems like a good idea to me, that we aver certain facts but do not get overly concerned if those facts are a little “off”. If, or as, we shift centripetally, in thought or on the ground so to speak, into focus on some point or other, we may get more anxious about the fragility of our wisdom, of its reality, of its truth.

The notion of fragility was to counter the not unreasonable argument that the meaning based on the apparent reality was internal to the organism, a feeling of anxiety or dread. The apparent reality in the here and now could be questioned by what Bickerton called the “naked reality” that we can only sense. We sense this naked reality but can never actually utterly know it as it “is”. This is simply a fact of our human condition, and when we swap opinions we would consider it reasonable that if we did bear down centripetally upon this point we would all agree that we believe what we sense is real enough, but is not the “naked reality” that we sense. If we bear down on the ground, on foot, the naked reality is perhaps more real, but the meaning might not be. For now, and more later, I will be calling this naked reality using the term synchronicity for reasons that I will try to make clear. This synchronicity is whatever it is, and thus can fail to be the that and how in the way I might expect. At that point some centripetal effort is required that may or may not restore the that and how to what is anticipated by the rules and axioms of that culture. Usually a culture is keen to ensure that centripetal efforts by feet on the ground or thought of that sort do actually result in relatively successful descriptions of the that and how of the reality we sense, if not of the synchronicity, which is as I put it, my term for “naked reality”.

Gadamer [1900-2002] studied with Heidegger in Freiburg in Germany, however he turned to interpretation, also called hermeneutics rather than understanding appearances. The difference is something that will take a while to comprehend for readers who do not know about hermeneutics. This is not a failure of education or intelligence on our part, as to our innate abilities as human beings. It is however a failure of our educational institutions who more or less have to teach fully explanatory cultures to children and novices of the fully formed cultures in any culture. The that and how a culture uses, as Hertz [1881-1915] wrote of in his book “Death and the Right Hand”, has to correlate with the consequences of synchronicity somehow, otherwise the “game is up”. The “game” in this sense is the authenticity of participation in the culture. The wise who teach that cultures require reasonable faith in their wisdoms by those who wish to participate in the culture whilst avoiding undue anxiety about naked reality.

As I think I understand it from the work of Dreyfus [1929-2017] Heidegger believed he had solved the problem of subject-object by describing the experience of living within a culture. Heidegger had included the concepts of the individual and the appearances of phenomena that became objects for individuals within a cultural milieu of appearances, taking individuals out of limbo. So the relationship between subjects and objects was cultural wisdom. And remember the failure of the culture to maintain meaningful relationships at all times was handled by using fragility as a concept, requiring faith and belief. Changes that occur in the here and now challenge the culture and the that and how of those challenges such as occur have to be accomodated and assimilated as part of being authentic in a culture. But we could add, that as Hertz suggested, the wise ones of that culture had to be on their toes so to speak. They had to deal with fragility so that the anxieties of their “flock” as to the meaningfulness of it all were quelled at least enough to get back to a normal fragility, a normal stability in which the “rules of authenticity” would apply. A sort of “expect so much but not more” kind of relationship between the wise and their “flock”. An existential quotient of faith we might call it.

On the other hand Gadamer worried that the individual might have more to do with the culture than Heidegger had allowed for. I too believe that Heidegger may well have ignored much of what individuals might be doing as processors of synchronicity, in part because as Jonas describes the situation in his work, Bultmann insisted on faith, pistis, rather than knowledge, gnosis. Gadamer too worried about knowledge rather than or as well as faith. My point on this is that if an individual is authentic because of faith in the culture, then the notion of the wise ones in that culture becomes more important than the individuals in the "flock". Most existentialists up to Sartre [1905-1980], [see for example Kauffmann's [1921-1980] book], took it those taking charge of wisdom might expect that faith in the culture was required of individuals in a "flock". A leap of faith is required in order to be authentic about a fragility that everyone, including the wise, must suffer because synchronicity is nakedly real, or rather naked reality is whatever it is, the wisdom is about the culture, and it is about being "right enough" so to speak. So participants must make a leap of faith, and remain brave, to some extent as in Nietzsche, for example, to hold on to the culture even in times of adversity. Without this "tolerance of faith and wise ones" the fragility required for the stability of a culture is existentially threatened.

In my opinion, having read Sartre a few times at different times in my life, Sartre was quite confused and confusing about the notion of culture because he seemed to be centripetally inclined to give opinions, ask questions, about the soul and/or the self. As Derrida [1930-2004] pointed out in his "On Spirit" Heidegger failed to actually deal with spirit in his work. Brentano [1838-1917] the psychologist was similarly interested in the soul rather than in culture per se. Rather than the self being this cultural being on the basis of faith and authenticity in that faith, Sartre seems to wonder about the role of the self and of perception and "the gaze". In some ways this undoes the work of Heidegger who thought he had welded subject and object together in culture. To be fair this was and is the belief of most of those involved in cultural studies and their historical myths and traditions seemingly aimed at helping the individuals in the "flock" comprehend the wisdom of the culture in some way, often seeming daft now, but at the time, centuries ago perhaps, pragmatic, even creative, in order to achieve stability amongst the participants in the culture. Gadamer's approach to the individual and knowledge, however, had more to do with gnosis, the study of knowledge, than to do with the soul of man. Thus for me Sartre takes his readers off to a vitalist spiritual position on this. Gadamer, and for that matter me, seem to want to ask about the reliability of knowledge itself. This after all is what we otherwise need to simply have faith about, whilst being aware that now and again faith is absolutely necessary to "bridge over" the occasional let down or fragility of the wisdom. My point here is that concerns about the soul are centripetal to the concept soul, whereas concerns about existential spread and framing are centrifugal to it and ultimately lead inexorably to limbo.

I like Gadamer's doubt about the approaches of so called natural science, the that and how of things, and also his doubt about authorship. I like that because after all Heidegger was trying to resolve the issue of subject and object. To merely push the problem to one or other boundary condition of synchronicity or wisdom is not a resolution of the problem of this authenticity that Heidegger requires of the individual participant in the culture. Synchronicity is the naked reality, wisdom is the "fragile" that and how of it. The hermeneutic approaches by everyone other than Gadamer, i.e see Bleicher's [extant] book, look for the author behind the culture, the author of the culture. Scientists as we know look for the here and now, the that and how objective reality of phenomena and related behaviours. In the sense of the culturalised individual Heidegger's theory seems to work, but only when it works so to speak. The doubt comes particularly when and if we ask where cultures came from in the first place.

So I will end this first essay by making a suggestion about how we should consider the concept of the culture. And I am going to suggest here that rather than consider the culture as a thing, which of course it can appear to be as a phenomenon, and as a wisdom of the that and how of it, that we consider the culture as a "project". Like cultures, projects have beginnings and endings. This requires that we have conversations and can move towards and away from an epicentre of project x, thus centripetally and centrifugally as we seek to clarify our conversations or open them up. Thus centripetally towards a robust fragility of agreement, and centrifugally away from such an agreement and towards the limbo of more general conversations.

History as Reason

In this second essay "**history as reason**" I discuss how diarising the that and how of experiences produces our concepts of both tradition and change out of limbo, but restricts us to the project.

-

I ended the previous essay with the notion that we can assume that like projects, cultures have beginnings and endings out of and back to a fleshy limbo. A project can have leaders, they need to be wise, and followers are required to have faith in their wise leaders in order to protect the project against entropy. The big advantage of our languages, our human languages, is that we can invent anything we wish to point at, the that and how of it, the what where and why of it, simply by producing a word for it that needs relatively few elements, Bickerton [1926-2018] writes that we use a few entities to create an infinite number of entities. In some ways what scientists often strive to do, as a practice is to experience phenomena doing deeds in the here and now and then repeat those deeds until there is no variation in the outcome of those deeds. Scientists can then describe the that and how of what happened as reality with some certainty of it being true of appearances, the naked reality remaining merely sensed or measured by us in this "fragile certainty". They cannot actually say for certain it is true as they describe it for two reasons. One is that the description is not the deed itself, the other is that even the deed is felt by the senses rather than known as the naked reality, which is this synchronicity of mine. Another quite big issue that I will get on to in later essays is that describing the here and now of what happens, apart from not being anymore the actual here and now but a description, we describe just part of whatever synchronicity is as a universe or symbiotic relationship to our species. The description is ineluctably personal or social so to speak.

In some ways Heidegger [1889-1976] has already "solved" the middle or pragmatic problem for those who care to explore his work or read Dreyfus [1929-2017] on the work of Heidegger, and Husserl [1859-1938]. for that matter. The sense of what happens is to be considered a fragile and faith based certainty as to its relationship to personal and social "reality". But the first problem of the description is serious for all of us when joined up to the third, the completeness of the description as part of the universe, or part of reality as a whole linked to description. Even scientists were prone to believe, after Comte's [1798-1857] positivism, that if they all created a project called scientific practices, they could complete a description of the universe that would work as a subject-object correlation of synchronicity to description. Heidegger was after all describing or theorising on what happens in traditional cultures. But of course as Borges' [1899-1986] notorious joke, a one to one map of the terrain, Magritte's [1898-1967] "treachery of the image" [or description], and Bateson's [1904-1980] "Ecology of Mind", have noted, there is an actual impossibility of knowing the absolute reality of what is described such that describing more of it is not going to make much difference to the accuracy. The point is the "middle" of personal and social faith in "opinion". The description must act as a "strong" or "weak" theory of opinion, honest and dishonest. Thus whilst we can commit descriptions to naked reality, synchronicity as I call it, the description has to be considered as a project which acts in the way Heidegger suggested a culture acts. One social scientist has a theory about theories which is along the lines of strong and weak theories that are strong and weak according to the support they get. Bloor [1942-].

So the problem we seem to have now is that the that and how of descriptions are maintained by scientists and teachers and descriptions that individuals have to be authentic towards, i.e. have faith in, without expecting too much, that are mostly very much like what was known as a "langue" – de Saussure's [1857-1913] anecdotal opinions [using language] used to describe the that and how of the project. So by adding Bloor's concept of strong and weak we can notice that an opinion can be "popular" and "unpopular" and also strong and weak, each term seemingly promiscuous as to its partner, as to its popularity and also its veracity; i.e. a description that creates anxiety but is popular, so weak yet strong, and so on. [These projects become flutters of butterflies later in this book].

In terms of a culture the notion seems to be quite strong and popular, for example, that there was some sort of historical beginning of it back in antiquity. The same would be true if the culture was a project although it may not be popular to use the term antiquity for a project. The notion is the same however. At some moment, in this synchronicity of mine, there is a that and a how and a description of it such that there is a, or several, subject-object bondings. The beginning of the project would be some descriptions seminal to what might become "the project". These would describe the that and how of it. The project proceeds as it may in synchronicity. The description grows part by what we may call "grace and favour", or evolution, or synchronicity, the fact that it just does, and part by the that and how, the cause and effect we might say. The wise ones check it for tolerance and the followers also check it for its utility and fragility in use and in addition follow their leaders wisdom as to the overall descriptions that are now growing up as this new project, or old revived project, whatever, but all projects are anecdotal.

So this is perhaps when to explain synchronicity. My idea of this is that it seems to me that we are all on planet earth together in the here and now symbiotically as a species. The that and how of it is of course diverse around the globe because the globe is spherical and we are dispersed all over the spherical surface. Symbiosis is like a conversation between our species as a whole and the earth as all of us relate to synchronicity chemically, which of course includes our individual attitude to what appears to us individually. Nonetheless there is an immediacy about the diversity within the here and now such that we have conversations with each other, but are obviously limited in that regard. These conversations are free to wander as they may which is centrifugally and centripetally, the latter then become projects limited by the conversion of conversations into communications as cyclic feedback rather than just processing per se.

So synchronicity is for me just an acknowledgement of the genetic link between us all which seems to have been understood by for example Darwin [1809-1882] but better understood by lthe later Fodor [1935-2017] who realised the importance of the need to study the individual rather than the project in terms of where projects, like cultures, come from. The later work of other scientists provided the extraordinary findings that Feynman [1918-1988] called QED, quantum electrodynamics, which allowed him to describe the universe as a sort of chemical milieu, a complex of consequences of chemical and electrical actions or behaviours that gives rise to genetics, and epigenetics, see the Carey [extant] book on that, and the development of complexity theory as described by say Mitchell [extant]. This synchronicity of mine then is the immediacy of our symbiotic relationship to fluidity rather than to our planet which converts to the synergy between each individual existing within synchronicity. This suggests that the immediacy could be considered as a chemical, almost fluid milieu. I will develop this concept in later essays since it is probably as new to you, as indeed it is to me although I have been playing with it for a while now. Yet out of this immediacy and then fluid chemical relationship everything that we know, all the thats and hows of the universe appear to us according to our relationship to those appearances. This includes the later emergence of words as elements and facts about them [ontics, butterflies], words as phenomena like all other phenomena in principle.

For a long while, for us humans, trying to comprehend common notions of what was real seemed like a positive completion project started by Euclid [mid 4th–mid 3rd century BC] as a development from basic numbers, maths, and algebra, symbolic arrangements of categories, i.e. languages, to an interest in shape, volume, area and so on. This ability to comprehend some "projects" of the chemical milieu, as we can see in our "built environments", became too much to keep quiet about so to speak when extended into astrology as astronomy. The notion that one of our own projects, the clock for example, could be converted into a time machine for the convertion of synchronicity, as in the International Meridian Conference in October 1884, almost global time, although it was not called that, just the that and how of synchronicity, that managed to describe the that and how using verbalisation and marks on a map that developed into words used to increase the benefits of the descriptions we could make by increasing the ability of some of us to make descriptions. For example I have often thought of cave drawings as schools for hunters, say, who were at that time a sort of brotherhood, perhaps sisterhood who knows, that shared secrets about hunting, or perhaps just about painting on walls. The hunting secret society sort of idea appeals to me.

The point about this is that we convert the synchronicity and its fluid chemical make up, into appearances that have shape and form and personal and social relativity of location and part/whole as to the relationships between the appearances and the descriptions of the that and how including words. We create forms and essences. Thus we manage to convert our descriptions of that and how from mere processing of things sensed, things felt and things thought, to things done, as well as the that and how of things done that we could just remember. That includes words, so from fluid to things, elements, facts about elements, ontics, feedback, in which words were phenomena along with all other phenomena.

Hubris and excitement, masked or tamed as this ability to make a sensible opinion out of word phenomena that had acquired shape and form and relevance out of this fluidity of mine, aka, "rationality" has became despotic as a theory. Thus the new science as both empirical, Bacon [1561-1626] and historic, Vico [1668-1744], so, empiricism leading to "natural" or "human" science, and history of languages [aka society-semiotics] and thus "natural" meaning, rolled out as some say, the two versions that later became the Viennese and Frankfurt schools as natural science and social science, generally speaking. The one dealing with systems, the other with languages assuming social systems following the antiquities in terms of the social project of societies. The one a natural order, the other also a natural order. The Cosmopolis as Toulmin [1922- 2009] refers to this hubris of the reading writing dilitante wise persons who had gradually become professors in universities. The apparently unnoticed hubris here is the hubris converting anecdotes into a universal project.

Sadly the Berlin "school" of Humbolt [1767-1835] seems to have not got such a popular uptake for his "Theory of Human Education" "wissenschaftslehre", the "science of knowing" which remained mired in episteme and not perhaps "daring" to investigate the Fichte'an [1762- 1814], theory of the individual solipsistic soliloquising isomorphic bonding of reality to description using a language system, since Marx [1818-1883] had linked Fichte to "german idealism" as the opposite to materialism. In that, as Kolakowski [1927-2009] noted Marx did us no favours as it turns out because the words are in effect much more our sorts of materials and material in terms of noises and marks made by humans quite specifically as to making them into systems because so fecund in terms of possibilities of articulation and production. Neither indeed did Humbolt's sibling [1769-1859] fare much better in his attempt to "roll out" a complementary "climate change" model of the chemical milieu as an "organic milieu", the chemical milieu, closer to the fluidity of synchronicity, which now others are also taking up as a possibility, such as Kauffman [1939-] for example. The notion of organic as the reference to its own production of the parts used in systems solving the problem of the authorship of the many cultures that seem to have "lives of their own", as do we as individuals. This transposes easily onto the concept of the project as culture. This turns out to be a fundamental error, the hubris of theology.

The project is the product of some synchronicity that becomes part of the that and how of behavioural practice of an organism that can also describe it within centripetal and centrifugal conditions of being. When this description is marked in some way that can be shared by other organisms the behavioural practice can spread by mime and remembering for example. When the description is marked by word and writing, and unique to an organism, us, the behavioural practices become unique to us. As they develop the effect in synchronicity is to make the individual synergy lean towards a new culture of language as specifically human. This seems to apply best to promiscuous languages that are not fixed. Thus as an academic language, english has fared better than say german or french. Conversations [centrifugal conditions of being] are easier allowing novel centripetal conditions of being to emerge as new understandings by shifting the epicentre of project "x". Thus we can have anecdotal projects and social projects using anecdotal projects.

The "world of the description of the project" as we might call it is forced to face up to the "world of the practice of the project" because if the two do not merge synchronously, do not correlate, the project is no longer developing as one, but as merely a conversation. This produces the sense of history or antiquity of the project and also a sense of old and new practices or timeless practices of centripetal and centrifugal social shiftings. Ontic readings, knowing about entities and the facts about them in "any built or made subject-object relationship" become problematic in the 20th century when Goldstein [1878-1965] for example, having had his hands on the here and now of the that and how of actual brains averred that we do not "see" ontics, or entities, per se. Brunswick [1903-1955] the psychologist attempted to settle the question of what is commonly referred to as perception, and analytical synthesis [analytical hermeneutics] of what is "perceived". He found, after an exhaustive study that individuals are more likely to "perceive" what they believe to be correct than what is really there for them to process.

So what we should in my opinion notice from this is that since we started to produce projects the projects we do have shifted from those described by a limited number of wise persons with inevitably a large number of peasant followers doing the agricultural work, to a lot of wisdom about the project being in the form of ancient or previous to the here and now texts. The resolution of incommensurability between old but "valuable" texts and new descriptions of practices in the here and now would remain with wise persons, whilst conversations and opinions aplenty could be carried on generally. A few burnings and hangings could prevent new, unwelcome, projects from developing further than their shifting of the epicentre of project "x". Where a propensity to social convergence towards any specific anecdotes occurs, the flock accepts the "shepherd".

What had happened is that a large amount of written material had grown exponentially. This required specialists to deal with it. The point I wish to raise is that in effect a large number of new projects had emerged all of which it seems follows the Heideggerian model of cultures erroneously. The subject-object bond is made by using descriptions that correlate to practices that must remain adequate enough to keep wise persons and followers in stable enough relationships using shared anecdotes. The effect is to either grow projects developmentally or to proliferate the number of projects, all of which have quite similar features even though the practices and descriptions are not the same and to a great extent incommensurate between projects. The main point to note is that the reason for incommensurability is that as a project emerges from fluidity it acquires appearances that have to remain, battle for survival we might say, in relation with all other opinions, projects, anecdotes. Words of all sorts, articulated appropriately, allow descriptions of all sorts to be commensurate with the that and how of everything. What makes a project a project is the eidetic shift towards its epicentre leading to the emergence of understanding the anecdote. The epicentre is an epiphenomenon, i.e. not an entity but an appearance that appears because of the behaviour of individuals who speak. Centripetal moves in "studios", i.e. conspecifics knowingly open to conversations, with synchronicity [and thus perhaps alone] allow projects to emerge because of the eidetic shifting to project x. Centrifugal eidetic shifts away from understanding are however encouraged by conversations rather than attempts at communicating as feedback to awareness of centripetal eidetic shifts. But "above" this the social epicentre can expect a large theological anecdote [but that is hubris].

Coherence

In this third essay "**coherence**" I discuss how the project can quickly become a record of a tradition that we can adhere to. In adhering to the project mechanics we maintain tradition, but are condemned to choose wisdom rather than play.

-

One missing issue in the first essay, above, was the shift in the Husserlian [1859-1938] idea of the life world, which Husserl later regretted, and the uptake of that idea as a human life world. This suggests that we humans are trying to imagine an existing reality. But as I explained in the first essay, the better theoretical belief, is that descriptions are variably related to the that and how of synchronicity by the work of those who make and then support the descriptions. This is what makes us different as humans since we support descriptions rather than requiring the that and how of synchronicity to support us. Our niche is the project not the commensurate part of the earth, although our symbiotic niche as verbalisers seems to have given us supremacy of the food chain almost completely save for a strong Malthusian [1766- 1834] theory on our propensity to be predatory and parasitic rather than commensalist, sharing amongst other species, about which more in other essays, other books, other opinions.

The term "langue" used by de Saussure [1857-1913] was the project as a whole, so like the "systems" of scientists who historically began to try to describe synchronicity by describing their own experiences of what appears as space and time to the rest of us as if peers, produces a project that is the correlation of material and space and time correlated to material descriptions. But as I explained there is a big difference in the fragility of opinions in conversations and the ontics, the entities and facts about those entities, required for the robust fragility of the firmly epicentred project.

The scientific project as we know ran up against some of the cultural projects, especially some of the cultural projects we call religions. One imponderable was the question of the soul since the material correlations of systems to systems did not need one. What is mysterious about epicentres is, as I have explained, that they do not exist other than as the result of the behaviours of iindividuals moving towards or away from that epicentre. The way to do this is to move towards an ontic condition in which entities and facts about them are correlated to a system of words creating a robust fragility that is project based. Or, to move away from an ontic condition in which conversations and opinions are freely voiced but are fragile in their correlations to the that and how of synchronicity. Of course those conversations can be robustly fragile as to the that and how of a son, or daughter, or a stranger, or anything at all really, such is the nature of conversations; they are the "stuff of the life of a verbalising creature that we are" unless you prefer solitude and practices of self sufficiency.

The notion of faith does of course play well into both opinion giving and fact finding, both of which are fragile, the one truly fragile, almost chance perhaps, or anecdotal, the other studied, peer reviewed we might say, robustly fragile. The two "moves" have become unnoticed it seems because the notion of the individual as interpreter of synchronicity was promoted by it seems Kant [1724-1804] and his concept of synthesis through the processing we do in his Copernican [1473-1543] revolution. In doing this he promoted an opinion about individuals that has been correlated to the term "enlightenment" in which we enlighten ourselves as to being in the world by seemingly peer reviewing the world individually and collectively. From what you have read in this book you should by now know that that is impossible. But if you have been educated, which we all have been, in order to read and write, then most of us believe we can indeed peer review the universe, or at least the world.

Peer review, as you know, means a review by equals. This is the common opinion about the enlightenment as it is often called that emerged out of Kant's work. It is by the way solely responsible for the nonsense of the invisible hand, or natural peer review, or peer review of the economic system that has allowed project "rob the masses" to proceed as far as it has. When 1% of a fragile opinion is supposed to become a robost fragile project known as the economic system of the 100% then it should be obvious how wrong this peer review of synchronicity is. Hegel [1770-1831] had a go at correcting synthesis by trying to establish a peer review at a national scale, however peer review is about an epicentre not a thing. Thus Hegel appears to be asking us all to believe in a vitalist spirit. Derrida [1930-2004] in my opinion, does the same thing when he asks Heidegger about the basis upon which Heidegger's claim about faith "in" a set of behaviours is based. It is, as I have explained, based on "there being", ha, an epicentre to the project in which people "cohere" in seeking a robust fragility to their description of synchronicity. In my opinion Hegel was correct in noticing the necessity of a project. He may or may not have included the issue of master servant in his work but seems to have done in his writing. Thus the notion of masters, peers of the realm so to speak, and servants, having conversations between them, works quite robustly in a fragile way on that. as Machiavelli [1469-1527] wrote in a robustly fragile way the relationships between masters and servants, or peers and conversationalists is a notoriously fluid one, yet stability is required for political economic continuity and thus the establishment of traditions by establishing the project of identity. In Hegel's case this was of the German state I believe. The same is true, however, of any project. The peer review amongst those [any individual who wishes to become a peer] who become peers, become peers by literally feeling their way towards the epicentre that does not exist. What exists is the search for a fragile robustness in the correlation between synchronicity and the that and how of phenomena, and the that and how of the words used obviously makes correlations, and communications, an improvement on the more fragile opinions in conversations that can be had by any one of us on the planet sharing the same dictionary, grammar and syntax. A promiscuous language like english has fewer problems in allowing conversations to meld into peer review, it seems from the use of english in academic work [although most people seem to blame transport and mercantile projects as if sacks of corn can create such a fluid morphology between mime, through opinion, and anecdote, to peer review and adoption for a project, on their own without us!].

In this synchronicity that we are all included within, it seems, we are all together. But bodies have the effect of separating us from each other and putting us into the position of the forest animals amongst the knowledge trees of cause and effect and grace and favour related groups. The surroundings we are grown up in are quite often relatively stable, not always but often enough. The surroundings we occupy as adults used once to be either nomadic or domiciled. Even if nomadic the "wanderers" were often cyclical and seasonal, cultivating various knowledge trees of the two "types", grace and favour, which is the emergence of a phenomenon out of fluidity, the fragile, and cause and effect once we can sense some sort of phenomenon as a that and how relationship, the robustly fragile. This is a common experience over vast areas of the surface of the earth. The empiricists Locke [1632-1704], and Hume [1711-1776] struggled with this and then Kant believed, I believe, he had solved it with his notion of universal processing. But he had in fact fragmented the project of understanding the universe. Rather than one earth, one theology, synthesis takes "centre stage". Fragility is the apriori [fate], robust fragility is pistis, tempting fate, gnosis.

It was I believe Uexkull [1864-1944] who came up with the human life world, and Husserl who popularised, to his later regret, the life-world concept. This put synchronicity as the project epicentre which is profoundly unhelpful because synchronicity is the fluidity of the chemical milieu, of existence itself. I believe Husserl's regret was because the concept had been wrongly imagined both by his readers and himself and by the later, common form of conversational hermeneuts. The world imagined could not it seems be imagined as anything other than as one that could be described because we are verbal organisms.

So the authorship of synchronicity is not the question. If context then who sets the boundary that context requires? Who determines the limit to what can be included? Who sets the limit to what should go where and when? Who halts the whole process of adjusting the arrangement of things, of Kant's synthesis, of Hegel's peer review and conversational delight amongst the servants of the peers? All in the name of stability and then tradition, pre Kantian, pre science, fragility and faith, post Kantian, scientific fragility and knowledge.

The notion of diachronous comes with the completion of the cultivation of a fully developed system of language as per de Saussure's "langue". The desire of a "person" to be wise about the universe itself, to know as well as the next about that and how, to be able to be the same as a peer and yet remain content as a servant seemingly related to the verbalists access to this stuff called knowledge. We can still see this claim stuck upon the exterior wall of the british library as I write, to our shame, since it is a woeful misunderstanding of what knowledge is. Yet we adhere to Kant's error, as it should be called, as Meillassoux [1967-] also I believe calls it, so it is not just me. We adhere to it because it seems that if language is a structure correlating entirely to synchronicity [which remember I claim is fluid] then we can all, eventually, become peers.

But the chemical milieu is almost unknowable and the memories we have of our existence are unique and similarly subliminally connected up to the synchronous existence that we have where existing is within the CM, the chemical milieu as synergy between the organism we are and the chemical milieu itself, where most of the articulatory practices are subliminal.

The articulations of individuals intended as a socialisation can create conversations. These are certainly easier using a shared dictionary, but the projects are not based on context. This is the big mistake. The context that I taught appears to be a rationalised bounded set of ontic [an entity about which there are facts and features to know] entities about which there are facts and features that have to be known. But the "have to be" is this move I have described, within synchronicity itself, towards or away from "the project" [and as I will explain in other essays there are more than one of these to contend with]. Thus the move is towards conversations or peer reviews. The move is towards an epicentre that is cohered to as an epicentre by the peers in the peer review, who become peers on that basis, of participation in the move towards the project, or away from it and its peer group outcomes.

If you find this difficult then worry not since I have found it almost impossible during the past years right back to my puzzle over the way architecture is practiced, through my science masters and psychology doctorate, and then teaching cultural context. The big point in this essay is the coherence of peers reviewing the "move towards and away from the project" as the intention to participate in this project to produce a robust fragility of an understanding of synchronicity relative to the relevant project or not. Using a common dictionary is sometimes not enough, new words are needed, the point is the correlation to the that and how within any project. Meanwhile the world, the human world, is full of countless and often extremely fecund conversations, in which opinions about our symbiosis with synchronicity and about our projects are freely given and freely ignored, or not. The main point is that Kant removed Earth from "project being". Humans as the x of project being, the chosen ones in an ecological Eden, that ended with the robust fragility of knowledge as faith in science. Then the return to faith as natural science and neo Kantianisms. The point however, is fragility.

The Idea of the Eidetic

In essay four “”**the idea of the eidetic**” I discuss how typically the discussions arising over our relationships to an adherence to tradition and any desire for change have been forced into rhetorical agonisms. The clarity of the argumentation depends on the ability of both sides to “see the argument” amongst what are actually at least two, usually many more separate “projects” set against a relatively coherent background of conversations wherever we go.

-

So my purpose in bringing you here to this fourth essay of mine in this book is to emphasize the lack of context and the actuality of a completely invisible epicentre to any project worth its salt. By this I mean worth the effort to clarify the ontic, the ontic being the facts about entities and the entities required in order to make the project “real”. By “real” I mean robustly fragile, and by that I mean correlate to synchronisation and the synthesis we are able to do as humans. This fact seemingly of synthesis or processing we do is however, as you will now know, if you have read the previous three essays, or worked that out for yourself, a fragile synthesis and works as your own processing. The processing is yours alone. It is sort of like the processing of other humans, in fact a lot like theirs in general, the emergence of organisms out of synchronicity being governed it seems by something some call epigenesis, see Carey [extant] for an exegesis on this, so conspecific as to genes, then developed by epigenesis and learning. This breaks the continuity between parents and children as if merely a reproduction of the "persons".

As I have explained the synthesis, or processing we do, is similar amongst the mass of humans symbiotiocally upon what appears as the earth but is synchronicity as we know it. Thus a dictionary will have a common set of words and the grammatical rules and syntactic relationships of those entities will be sort of commonplace to us all. The exactitude of the rules will, as we know, depend upon this shift I have mentioned towards for example the project of conversations or peer review of a project. This gives rise to a lot of conversations about how the dictionary and the grammatical rules and syntactic relationships should be used. This is in and of itself an example of the morphological nature of our "immersion" in synchronicity, our synthesis of what emerges from synchronicity, phenomena, and our moves towards using langauge as a means of conversing or peer reviewing, and something else.

The something else is not just peer reviewing per se. As I mentioned already above, in essay three, and especially after Kant [1724-1804] and his concept of synthesis through the processing we do in his Copernican [1473-1543] revolution, we can all become peers. The real issue is peers reviewing what?

The what we review as peers is not conversation, nor is it necessarily or at all communication. The notion of communication has been established by Shannon [1916-2001] and Weaver [1894-1978] in the relationship we have when using transport rather than the feelings we have about synchronicity. The transport in their case was the telephone line and this has been extrapolated and expanded into the use of any medium in which transactions along some noise free form of transport are possible in a back and forth manner. This, as you will know, improves any peer review process as to the contents of what is transported, a sort of tick box check of the phenomena involved and the order in which the phenomena are arranged. In conversations that have become peer review back and forths, cycles if you wish, then they are no longer conversations but peer review. Note that the project is irrelevant in this. The concept of back and forth, of checking entities and their attributes as facts in the “lorry” or “cable” can extend to bytes or bits along a wire and back again. Often the cycle is left out, especially as the concept became misunderstood and was applied to descriptions given by masters to servants. The same mistake is made, as you know, in so called education where teachers mistakenly transport words and diagrams to students as if the mere fact of transport is enough to create in them the understanding that they are now supposed to be peer reviewing an entire disciplinary project. In my experience very few students have the confidence to think that, and the job of the teacher is to encourage that confidence in their students. This entails recognising the epicentre of the project and its boundaries, neither of which exist without the eidetic shifting.

Thus what peer review ought to be is the moves they make towards making their own project clear to each other. This is by way of conversations using words that come from the same dictionary, or are translated from other dictionaries. Occasionally translations are difficult. Reading Heidegger in english is a laugh because caveats about the impossibility of understanding the precise use of many german words crops up a lot, as if that is the point of it all, a precise translation from the german. The point is to become part of the same project. That we are all able to do, if we wish to do so and indeed if we are free to do so. Mind you the same applies to the work of Habermas [1929-] as to clarity of terms. And of course the individuals want projects of their own perhaps, and so force conversations on others, a never ending issue.

So making the project clear, eidetic, [and allowing for many conversations over the dictionary definition of eidetic as often happens, tirelessly it seems] is a process not only of Shannon and Weavering the "rationalised" entities, with attendant facts and attributes about them, into some project boundary that then represents the sum of the parts that is now other than just the sum of the parts. This is the sort of nonsense the Gestaltists came up with. Thanks to my awe of them I have been struggling with that for decades and so have most all of the existentialists and most "phenomenologists" who have rather taken to the Gestalt eidetic and this "other than" and "more than" nonsense. There is some use in the principles of proximity, similarity, continuity, and connectedness as to correlating the that and how of synchronicity to the that and how of syntax and grammar and the project of choice. But the principle of closure is nonsense if you believe in synchronicity, which of course you perhaps do not but I do.

Why is it nonsense? Because it is seriously misleading those who take it as gospel that there is a context to be protected that is more than, other than, just the sum of parts, as if there is a covenant between synchronicity and our species. Planners for example claim that "harm" is caused to a cultural context, or a building, by some entity or other that has not previously been in that building or tradition. Harm to who? The harm is to their own feelings about their own project whatever that is, and we can come to that in another essay later in the book. The building, as far as I know, has no feelings. The context does not even exist, at least not in my theory although in the theories, i.e. the verbal conversations and peer reviews put up by said planners, there will be words and images as entities in conversations that do indeed "pain" the theorizers because it harms their own project, and often the project is their own person as an expert on cultural context or tradition or what not. They have an Erasmus syndrome.

Thus in terms of symbiosis, of the whole of our species in synchronicity, any clarification of a project depends upon the moves made towards that clarification by us individually. Thus I can clarify my own projects, and you can yours, or we can decide to start clarifying joint projects such as when we fall in or out of love. The driver is as several neuroscientists put it, such as Damasio [1944-], our feelings. The synthesis as Kant correctly noted is the processing we do, as Damasio explains, and that processing is essentially between what I call PMI and PMII. This is my "translation" of Damasio's liking, I believe, of gut and the mid brain, and the integrating nervous system that, for example, Greenfield [1950-] writes a lot about. Now their conversations, their books, are not communications, since there is no back and forth, believe me if you write to them they will give you polite replies via a "hellper" such is academe and its corridors. As Wilde [1854-1900] put it I believe, like the Ritz, the academic world is open to all, implying that if you were well off you probably actually had more chance than if poor. Money opened the doors of the Ritz and of academe, but in fact it is not so much money as the project of peer review which is indeed, as I have said, the project of projects, what they are and how they are formed. Because of Kant's insistence on a synthesis of common properties of existence he condemned us to years of mistaken struggle.

So PMI for me is understood by Merleau Ponty's [1908-1961] I think posthumous work taking flesh as the materiality that matters most to us in terms of what appears in relationships to what is imagined. My PMII is understood by for example many neuroscientists, such as LeDoux [1949-] who describes the integrating brain as a synaptic galaxy which is in effect very difficult to comprehend as a thing so much as an ongoing process. So my argument is that the feelings, for example as explained by Pert [1946-2013] are actually the emergence of feelings from the synchronicity between PMI and PMII that relate to synchronicity itself as a whole [that we cannot possibly know about in total according to me and Feynman [1918-1988]]. And I am sure you possibly do not agree but that is, literally, another conversation. In the peer reviewing that I did on this in my PhD and then subsequently, the project of understanding projects works just fine with that sort of arrangement. Synchronicity, PMI relating to PMII such that behaviours are related to feelings the whole time we are awake and alive. When asleep I have read that the integrating brain and the gut are still having conversations, behind our backs so to speak.

Merleau-Ponty had this idea I like about the blind man's stick becomes part of the "flesh" of the blind woman/man. To me this is an example of existential conversations about touch and "matter" linked to the emotions of an individual, the blind woman/man and the difference between me, for whom a stick is another emergence from synchronicity that is this or that, or probably because of its handle and colour and appearance the stick of a blind person, but it is probably not flesh to me, but is to the blind person. The point of this is I think to emphasize the way in which we can understand the "harm" done to our feelings when we understand an entity in a particular way. The driver is the emotions, and the point is to try to figure out how the emotions drive individuals towards and away from the epicentre of a project, any project, driven by feelings about synchronicity and emergent verbalisations driven beyond boundaries [to previous or other understandings].

So the idea of the project that I want you to understand, and that I am trying to understand myself, is the emotional drive to find some epicentre in which a set of relationships not only seems to emerge out of the fluidity of synchronicity, but does so in such a way that my PMI and PMII create emotions I like rather than dislike. Pert wrote that this internal fluidity she describes is relatively a new kid on the block so to speak. Part of the mechanism of the conversation between PMI and II is the breathing we do it seems, and the blood pumped round by our beating hearts.

Of course once we are able to verbalise we are much more "equipped" to verbalise our relationships to synchronicity in a way we might prefer. The preferences may at first depend upon our feelings, and then upon the emergent features of synchronicity that occur around and about this fleshy thing we call a body. And of course this fleshy thing takes on some sort of appearance. It also takes part in conversations and on many occasions projects that are none of our own but imposed upon us by others, some of our own apparent appearance and others much bigger than us, adults of all sorts, shapes and sizes. And we find, quite often if not always, that the articulations of words can have a greater or lesser effect upon the articulations of what emerges out of synchronicity around and about us. In other words the around and about us alters, sometimes correlated to the around and about us of words that correlate to conditions we prefer, or to conditions we do not prefer. And I believe Merleau-Ponty was on to this in his "visible and invisible" the notion of what can and must emerge out of synchronicity and our many conversations is it seems often related to the ways in which we indulge conversations as opposed to communications. The latter are what many adults tend to encourage as the transport of emergent features of synchronicity, as words and that's and hows such that we do as we are told, as if part of some project or other that we actually like, rather than, if communication, some robot or slave that must obey the commands of its master.

So the notion of language as simply another emergence of words from synchronicity allows us to imagine languages per se as projects that seek to correlate to making a dictionary, thus semantics, and grammar, and syntax, to the needs and requirements of the users of it in correlating verbalisations to the that and how of entities and ultimately to understandings that are robust and fragile. We can furthermore aver that all projects go in two directions, centripetally towards an imaginary epicentre acting as an invisible beacon that in fact does not exist yet is “felt” by those shifting centripetally in their conversations, because the feelings are indeed felt. And centrifugally away from ever getting a project underway because the conversations are not turning into a peer review of the link between feelings and accomplishments that are required in order to make a project appear to “work”. In addition I must add that whilst miming and improvising can achieve some working outcomes on a spontaneous basis the use of verbalisations and thus additional correlations between the feelings of individuals and the other behaviours of participants seems to produce the effect of projects that are more robustly fragile than constant sponteneity can do. In other words at some point the recognition that a project exists, as a set of behaviours felt to be liked by participants, can become a sort of indentity for those participants and perhaps the emergent features of processing on the part of other organisms is able to sense that such projects exist when they do indeed emerge out of synchronicity, see Johnstone [1933-] on this phenomenon. Our species use of langauges do of course allow the emergence of at least part of the project, the verbal parts, that may be well correlated with the that and how of it, such that the project becomes visible so to speak, even though it is not actually in the here and now other than as a set of words or images as in fact words can be.

Bickerton [1926-2018] has even suggested that language forms a secondary sensory world in which we know differently to the absolute sensory data we all process as conspecifics relating to surroundings without having the secondary sense to delude us. This also helps to explain how we can have over five thousand languages that we do not shift out of comfortably even though we have conspecific experiences of lakes, rivers, mountains, fire, earth, air, water and so on. So first niche for primary senses, then language and this understanding that can bear no references at all to conspecific experiences of the room we are in when making an understanding more robustly fragile.

The Model of Social Utopia

In essay five "**the model of social utopia**" I show how the eidetic condition of our rhetoric has produced what I feel is a mistaken impression in most traditions that each one of them can finalise their rhetorical agonisms and thus produce a utopia. This makes crossing cultures, disciplines and peer review conditions impossible in my opinion.

-

So for readers who have not read the earlier essays I have got to a point at which I argue there is a basic synchronicity that we can never know other than as it appears to us as phenomena emerge from it as they seem to do. We, however are immersed in the same phenomena from out of which we ourselves emerge as phenomena, which I think makes sense. So we are the same as other phenomena that emerge out of synchronicity thus it is impossible to completely or at all know existing in which we too are existing presumably as part of synchronicity itself.

I have reported on the scientific projects of for example Damasio [1944-], Greenfield [1950-], Pert [1946-2013], and LeDoux [1949-], writing that they seem to agree in principle upon the importance of the chemical flow that has conversations between PMI and PMII [these are my terms for flesh, PMI and the synaptic galaxy PMII]. I refer to PM as protein mass in relation to the synaptic galaxy because it is in fact rather like, for me, a set of worms joined up by electro chemical links that are named synaptic clefts, hence the synaptic galaxy of Le Doux. PMI is the flesh not quite as Damasio has it in his project, but in mine the protein mass as a whole is considered as linked to the integrating capabilities of the synaptic galaxy. Damasio refers to this as dynamic homeostasis, but the trouble I have with his project is that using such a term creates another phenomenon that seems to be "doing something".

Basically the project I am interested in is the one where at its epicentre is the belief that we humans as organisms are merely part of this synchronicity of mine out of which we and other phenomena emerge. The phenomenon that is us becomes known by the conversation between PMI and PMII and synchronicity in the same way that all phenomena become known. In my project then there is a conversation between each of us and every other one of us in this human species existing within synchronicity. I could argue that there are conversations between every other phenomenon however I tend to go along with Bickerton's

[1926-2018] project insofar as we are the only verbalisers and thus language users. This has the unique advantage that I can then suggest that synchronicity between us human individuals is a conversation of some sort if we want it to be. Otherwise we are miming and/or bashing into other phenomena as do phenomena generally. Like other animals we can presumably as they do use phenomena themselves to think with, so things sensed become things thought. We also share with some/many the things done and things felt. But in addition we have verbalisations.

Now it seems that phenomena of a certain sort or sorts can mime or articulate in their own ways as can we. By articulating we can relate the feelings I have already written about in other essays, above, by articulating flesh and bone and so shift ourselves nearer and further away from phenomena that make us feel good and/or bad. Other mammals in particular seem to be able to do this and we also seem to be able to do this. But for them that is about it in terms of flocking, shoaling, herding, tribing and other sorts of group activities. Their protolangaugues according to Bickerton and also according to Calvin [1939-] are not up to much when it comes to complex correlations with that and how. So Heidegger's [1889-1976] model is perhaps good for animals with protolanguages but no more. Perhaps his model of cultures is like a protolanguage in which many of the possibilities for conversations are prohibited, which is after all what it is like to be in a totalitarian culture.

Us lot with verbal diarrhea at times can find ourselves within such totalitarian cultures and happy or sad about that. But my argument has been that cultures are really projects and projects emerge out of conversations that have shifted towards becoming projects and have then actually become them. The process is of selecting descriptions matching the that and how of existing in that process. We do this in the same way we select for the existence of a river to cross or a berry to eat. I would add that it seems to take a bit longer to get the hang of a fully developed language, a lot longer to get to grips with one or a number of projects, and quicker to decide whether or not we are hungry [without necessarily or at all knowing that the "reason", the cause of our yelling at the age of a few months or days even, is that hungry is what we might be, or wet, or cold, or bereft and so on]. What we learn to do because we can learn to do it, thanks to epigenesis going ok, and the underlying genetics, is to verbalise quite complex things felt, things sensed, things done and things thought [but not until we have learned to do so, after age two years].

Thus verbalisation seems to challenge the project that Descartes [1596-1650] had about subject object. Fortunately Dreyfus [1929-2017] suggests that Heidegger believed he had solved the problem of subject-object by describing the experience of living within a culture. In my opinion this would work for any organism with a protoculture and so, as with most mammals, we find niches in which specific genes find their project "home". I reckon this is probably what went wrong with von Uexkull's [1864-1944] project of the human life world, and Husserl's [1859-1938] project who popularised, to his later regret, the life-world concept as if it would be possible to bracket phenomena so that we could verbalise them. This seems incorrect given the two worlds of primary and secondary senses having different dictionaries so to speak.

Because of the mistake I mention in an earlier essay, that being the shannon-weaver transport issue, mis-verbalised as an issue of understanding rather than an issue of shifting into project mode as to the back and forth of specifics when at that stage. The peer review stage I called it. The notion being that once the specifics become important then we have moved from verbal diarrhea about primary senses towards attempting some sort of common synthesis with what we have available as synchronicity and the fleshy and integrating parts of our bodies, the PMI and PMII as I refer to them. This is not dynamic homeostatic synthesis, and this is the issue I have with Damasio, and I have tried to tell him so, but see note on academic situations, above, earlier.

The use of dynamic homeostasis as a condition of the individual who knowingly has a feeling, say, is not the issue even though it may motivate the individual to try to do something about the issue verbally. The actual issue is the phenomenal relationship to synchronicity that has to be resolved completely. Phenomena have emerged, and they emerge as they do, but not just as they appear to us but as they effect the flesh and the synaptic galaxy in the process. This is why the analytical philosophers of the early 20th century had such fun at the expense of the early british Hegelians because they could touch one hand on another and say how real that feels [primary senses merged with secondary senses craftily], thus reality exists. That is not quite the effect of touch but yes, the processing does give rise to a distinct feeling that things sensed are not all internal to us but are a complex mix of internal and external. In my opinion even here we are better off if we stick to my term project. We can adopt the theory that we can have "project exterior" and "project interior" and also "project real". And what we find is that for example if say Bhaskar [1944-2014] suggested as he did a project for critical realism, say, then it gets into a pickle but nonetheless is a project. The project was "solved" by one of his followers but only by suggesting a return to Heidegger's pistis, faith, solution using a belief in being as designed thus avoiding having to deal with questions of cosmogony, and of the secondary sense and tertiary sense of "abstract value".

The problem with all projects that involve verbalisation is that the correlation between the that and how of the language that is formed enough to be "complete" is not complete enough to cover all the possibility of both itself, the langauge itself, and synchronicity itself. In addition remember in the very first essay in this book I remarked how the descriptions can be robustly fragile and fragile and even pretty poor correlations to what emerges from synchronicity because we can never truly know synchronicity [or reality and so on]. So any total understanding is simply not possible unless we have a project that is called "let's delude ourselves with this verbalisation" of things thought, the two not being necessarily or at all the same.

So my point is that if we individually or socially decide to start shifting a conversation from centrifugally opinionating towards centripetally aiming at some apparently epicentred and contextually bounded project then we must behave towards that project as best we can, individually and socially as "peers". This means both sensory and verbal articulations move in the direction of point x of project x towards a robustly fragile understanding amongst peers.

This project concept of meaning seems to me to overcome the problem of Derrida's missing spirit because the existential effort is made by those who want the project to "work". Remember the project itself is not boxed in by any context, neither is it "constructed" as if a kit of parts seeking to become a whole, or a player or agent seeking to make an "it" whole. It is this certainty against which I have found myself constantly rebutted when and if on the odd occasion wishing that synchronicity would "reveal" its purpose. That is not where meaning resides. In fact meaning resides in a no place realm that some have called utopia, because that seemingly is what the word "means" in a different language to this. In other words synchronicity and us produce phenomena that appear to us such that our relationship to them is that which Meinong [1853-1926] described. Our use of language provides us with a phenomenal milieu in which we can be centrifugal and centripetal as to moving away from and towards a peer project. The complexity of this plus and minus could be thought of I believe as arriving at us in that we exhibit our plus and minus as feelings and articulations of both verbal and fleshy entities including our own bodies. We can even turn our verbal entities into "fleshy", material, texts. In doing this as Simon [1916-2001] noted - had we not the ability to "write things down" we would be in a perpetual quandry as to the totality of it all, adding it all up. And again, to remind ourselves of my earlier comment about fragility, even our project real when it seems real has a fragile meaning that can be more or less robust, and thus more or less of a risk on which to bet, first appearances, then primary senses, then secondary verbal senses, then inevitable fragility as to understanding because dependent upon focus, x, and context, boundary, that are epiphenomena.

Thus my developmental existential phenomenal that and howness, depTH is an interpretation of the existence or lack of existence of the eponymous project that has not real "being" and yet is brought into existence by those moving to "create" it by shifting towards its epicentre. As Simon noted the amount of effort an individual might put into such a move seems related to the rewards obtained. And as McLuhan [1911-1980] suggested the functionality, the use of phenomena, does not discriminate between "media forms". The medium is the message so to speak as to what the project entails, yet sets the demands for knowledge of the that and how required to be a peer, thus emerges the social action described by Arendt [1906-1975]. We can begin to see all sorts of "conversations" entering the cycles that our processing of synchronicity does. Our ability to anticipate the outcomes of such processing cycles, and even discuss such anticipations, concerning epiphenomenal appearances is, to me, rather wonderful.

As you may have noticed the little homunculus in the head that Greenfield writes of as a problematic error for us after Descartes, as in the problem of consciousness, who [?] is at home, is no longer a problem as such. It is the processing cycles "wot do it". There is still room for such a project, but it is somewhat tamed since it stands alongside many other projects. The animal spirit that seems to reside in the niche project of the non verbal protolinguistic organisms, and totalitarian cultures, is shown to be a myth or a convenient reference to the common behaviour of the organisms involved which is really the same as the sort of arguments made by anthropologists and behavioural scientists about animals, or tribes, herds, and so on, the sorts of problems sheep have, a peer problem that has to be solved without butterflies, as war [Sunzi].

Thus any model of a social utopia is a project in relation to which individuals are required by verbal or non verbal means to shift towards descriptions of “understandings on the way to meaning” that are fragile yet some of which can be robost such that an epicentre emerges towards which participants in the project are seemingly directed by the “flapping of wings” once they become peers. Note that theological “shepherds” always drive their “flock” pell mell towards primary senses, sight, touch and sound, as one drives any other mammal that is not human, so we can be “driven” by a flutter of butterflies if unaware of the “verbal” issues.

The seemingness of the project can be halted at any moment it seems by the cessation of the shift centripetally and the beginning of a shift centrifugally. So towards understanding or away from understanding as meaning. PMI and II remain but the verbal phenomena are like butterflies [see cover illustration of Play]. The verbal terms I use, plus and minus, towards away from, are just as possible, the plus and minus preferably linked to actual feelings felt, and towards and away from as thoughts, things done, things planned even, desired, wanted, not wanted and so on but as peers, no longer free [since PMI and II are now “netting” lepidoptera]. The notion is of a verbal milieu in which conversations cause a project to disappear or to start, by shifting towards or away from a project or different project as to anticipated robustness or fragiligy of emerging understandings.

So the whole notion of society is hereby made ridiculous. The same for community other than as a head count of some project so called, or actually in operation and wanting to use the term for a flock of sheep. There is no community genie or social genie doing this work any more than there is a homunculus doing the work of the individual. Luhmann [1927-1998] after Maturana [1928-] and Varela [1946-2001], called the individual the maker of a "self referencing system" I believe in his work, but he was caught up in project "systems" as per Bateson [1904-1980] and that suggests a meaningful system rather than an existential shift towards becoming peers of meaning as an outcome, fragile yet robust, which is what I am aiming for in my own project here. Turner [1951-] approaches sociology with a project noting that individuals have brains and thus that this should matter in sociology. This ignores, however, Bloor's [1942-] theory of the strengths and weaknesses of flutters and findings. At the moment I have agreed with him via email that this should give the systemic modellers pause, and also agreed with him that it does not seem to do so, such is their project, they know who they are no doubt. And many neuroscientists that I quite admire are adamant that a map or model appears in the head or brains that makes it then really difficult to approach synthesis as a continual ongoing process of butterfly production that does not stop even when asleep.

Finally in this essay I should mention Edelman [1929-2014] whose writing I have found particularly helpful in the past. His work includes the concept of mental mapping but he does this as actual linking up the various general areas of the nervous system not as if some map of reality – more an intermediate layer or layers [as of the neocortex] of interconnecting axonal links that wax and wane, that "locate" in my terms lots of worms that get caught up in specific functions within the synaptic galaxy, with other areas so that worms from several locations or modules as some call them, work in synchronicity on several intermediate layers, possibly neocortical layers. Perhaps I should call them caterpillars? This fits well with my own project and the link to functionality and synchronous working, and to de Saussure's synchronous and diachronous as developmental learning by these "caterpillars" producing their butterflies in our heads. This is I believe part of this conversational milieu I have mentioned out of which I believe all sorts of projects get to emerge because of the synergy between the organisms we are and the conversational milieu itself and our ability to notice the appearances of both understanding and meaning from those appearances. The phenomenal milieu without verbalisations works I believe in the same way, with various organisms able to shape and use phenomena just as we do, but without verbalisations that seemingly make us top of the heap if that is the sort of verbalisation you like, if not bottom of the heap is a conversation that might be had if lionising the natural as non-human [which seems to me to be a significant error of faith/belief in a creator as opposed to a belief in synchronicity a la early Wittgenstein]. The projects implied and inferred would obviously, in my opinion, be different, according to peer group pressure, the biggest factor of which seems to be the denial of the effects of peer group pressure on the part of individuals both as putting it on, and taking it for granted or grinning and bearing it.

We have primary senses much beloved of theologians and phenomenologists in seminaries justifying pure faith. Then we have secondary senses as languages with dictionaries [not historical fictions]. Thus for this project of mine links to the posthumous Wittgenstein [1889-1951] who prepares us for the tertiary sense of "money values", "digital data" and abstract value that seems able to direct individuals towards the greatest of flutterings on a global "stage"; money value as an almost purely fluid value like the chemical milieu, but flowing through us as dripping or flooding yet capable of settlement as a material form for the purposes of peer review, the robust fragility as I am calling it.

Post Positivism

In essay six "**post-positivism**" I discuss what we must all do if we are to accept that the possibility of utopia is not only unlikely because of the fluidity of electrodynamics, but also because our attachment to the tradition and wisdom of a project makes us sclerotic.

-

So take the five earlier essays above, previously, as what I have been struggling with for around seven decades now; since 1944 in some ways, since being born. Specifically I realised something was wrong in 1978. I won't repeat all that here since it is written in my earlier work here, and in my books, and earlier academic papers.

What is wrong is this notion that there is some total understanding of the universe to be had, or had, as knowledge, already had by someone or some group, or to be had by someone or some group. This is I think obviously a little worrying, this idea that someone other than the individual worrying, has this superknowledge or is part of a group that has superknowledge. The chance that any one of us conspecifics might know everything was given up seemingly after Erasmus [1466-1536] the last scholar “to know everything” [actually just a mistake about what knowledge is, which is “what we know”]. See “the vocation of the scholar” by Fichte [1762-1814].

So my point is that it is of little use suggesting that we describe what we do, which I have sort of done in the earlier five essays, and then write as if this is not what we do, as if what we have been doing with this anxiety about the superknower or the supergroup as part of that understanding allows us to continue with the Erasmus project? That understanding is, if you accept what I have written earlier, the understanding of what we actually do, which is to render the knowledge project of positivism robustly fragile and located in a phenomenal milieu rather than an ontic condition of entities and facts about entities. The fragility is born out of the butterflies and flutters that are manifestations of our phenomenal milieu made “real” by our individual PMI and II organic outputs.

So you should be able to imagine that this is a problem in all the philosophy groups I attend in London. Without the benefit of a text the description of what we actually do does not get very far into a conversation because the individuals in philosophy groups generally are seeking wisdom. That means some superknowledge or supergroup that knows everything. So individuals of the "old beliefs" drag conversations off into projects that they actually care about. It may be project "Plato", or project "Reality", or project "History", and so on. Sometimes it is project "Self" when, for example, an individual wants to get centre stage so to speak and tell everyone what is what. Such individuals give birth to a fllutter. This may induce awe and wonder, or chaos, confusion, or bemusement etc.

So first off in this essay I feel it is necessary to note that I believe the old beliefs are best called positivist. In my own case I relate this to Comte [1798-1857]. Durkheim [1858-1917] who seemingly, along with Du Bois [1868-1963], Marx [1818-1883], and Weber [1864-1920], wanted to produce a science of society. Comte is spoken of by many, as the father of social science, and Durkheim as the pioneer who made the study of society "more scientific" which we might say is more of a project in a way that was possibly the reason that Boltzmann [1844-1906] killed himself when theologians masquerading as scientists did not appreciate what he, Boltzmann, was trying to do with his pioneering work. In effect he was trying to solve the problem of Maxwell's [1831-1879] demon. Look this up on wiki if you have never heard of Maxwell's demon, odds are you probably have not, so do that now or soon. This little demon takes hot molecules from warm water and puts them on one side of the sink, and takes cold molecules and puts them on the other side. Magically, because we do not know who or what this demon is, we now have hot separated from cold, because the demon can sense which molecules are hot, which cold, and give them directions. Magic. [this happens in a glass of warm water, hot top, cold bottom, sort of].

By pointing out the synchronicity inherent in molecules as if they are tiny organisms, an effect we can now include in conversations as “quantum mechanics”. Boltzman made any theological theory of a cosmic logic unreal rather than real. As Boltzmann found it is possible to create statistical models of very large numbers of individual molecules or atoms in rather the same way that Lonrenz [1917-2008] established a theory of climate change. In this conversation, this book, I would say this indicates that programs can be revealed by statistics as if snapshots of molecular action as if by a heat detector, a machine that augments our organic senses. But as Durkheim noted, one who used statistics to great personal advantage, and believed in theological explanations of psychology, the statistical model tells us little to nothing about what any individual “caught up” in those statistics is “thinking” [processing synchronicity as “data cycles”] able to abduct and transduce mechanically as well as organically.

Now in my earlier five essays in this book, I have said, to confirm this as a conversation, this book, that thinking does not really exist other than as a part of our intersensory conversations, as primary, secondary and [to be sorted out] tertiary, so phenomenal, butterfly ontic, then social. I believe that is an important difference and immediately those keen on project "brain", and especially project "mind" will be angry or pained or "hurt". In many ways I could say that Descartes [1596-1650] introduced project "thinking" as the subject object relationship that Heidegger solved for mammals it seems. I have opened up a conversation on that already as to the processing that occurs in synchronicity within our own intermediate stages of processing making this subject-butterfly relationship. Since we have very little if any "control" over our bodies as to beginning and end other than as project "me" then the synchronicity inside us and out seems to me to have more sway over our lives than anything else. Thus for me synchronicity is this electrochemical activity along the lines of Feynman's [1918-1988] quantum electro dynamics that produces all the chemical elements that we find around and about us as human beings. Because of various "projects" these end up as the houses, cars, planes, trees and so on we are somewhat familiar with in contemporary life. The real processing however seems to take place as primary, secondary and tertiary, and also in wormy parallel links worm to worm that are wriggling to produce the consequences of synchronicity, the butterflies. Thus as Libet [1916-2007] suggests we seem to have "free wont" rather than free will. I.e. there is a strong element of feed back, or cycles of performances of processing before those consequences can be dealt with.

Comte was seemingly a secretary to Saint Simon [1760-1825] who is said to have noticed the change in statistical patterns from project rural to project industrial. I say this industrialisation has now become the pattern of large scale domiciles in whole countries where industrialisation has been adopted. For example according to some figures from Oxford researchers [ourworldindata.org/blog] the ratio of rural workers to urban dwellers is 1:100 in project "england". Saint Simon is said to have been an early bird in noticing this shift from peasant to proletariat [as individuals working in industry came to be called seemingly by Marx [1818-1883] see Engels [1820-1895]. The etymology of the term is from the latin describing "a man whose only property is his offspring", so the term is not really appropriate to the contemporary project "individual", but that is another conversation]. The concept of project "accumulation of wealth" is perhaps relevant to project "individual" and is yet another conversational gambit in the move towards or away from the robustly fragile understandings we may seek in synchronicity. I can suggest the individual as a "free butterfly" carries all sorts of caterpillars in its legs that dig deep into the chemical milieu to produce perhaps billions more butterflies in due course influenced by PMI and II.

So I think we can see, you and I, that the concept of the project makes it harder to string a few "facts" together in order to make a decent metanarrative, or large narrative string of facts we call history of the world, for example Lyotard [1924-1998] who suggested with some regrets later, seemingly, that simple and especially grand narratives were suspect. This sort of suggestion was not actually new because there were already rejections of myths and legends for various reasons. Mannheim [1893-1947] for example in his “Ideology and Utopia”, wrote about, started up a conversation about, the rejection of theology and the introduction of peer review as a method. But that was in my opinion a big mistake, and the reason I say this can be characterised by the way in which Wittgenstein [1889-1951] ironically had pretty much a solipsistic time of it in his life by spending a large amount of time on his own. He seemingly suggested the notion that there is a universal interpretation a la Kant [1724-1804] or Berkeley [1685-1753], or some common sense understanding of nature, in his early Wittgenstein phase, but gave way to the later Wittgenstein as some common game played relative to some common articulatory practices or “langue” with the same players most of whom seem to have lived in Oxford. My point on this is that the cultivation of common articulatory practices includes the participants. Thus Moore [1873-1958] and Russell [1872–1970] [see Ayer] brutally rejected “idealist” butterflies creating a sort of butterfly producer that peer reviewed itself into an analytical mode of production, ironically spawning Wittgenstein in the process. This is my "peer review" stage of a "project" and its metamorphosis. Dewey [1859-1952] the pragmatist cottons on to this in his work considering "knowers and the known" as the necessity of a program, in my opinion, much more than did Dilthey [1833-1911], see Bleicher [extant] in his approach to interpretation a.k.a., hermeneutics and authorship, ultimately allowing theology in through the front door of that sort of understanding as "communication of certainty" rather than a peer review of conversations. The idea of "communicating with strangers" is in my opinion ludicrous as a description of what happens. I agree on this with Gadamer [1900-2002] as he critiqued Dilthey about the need to include the temporality of my synchronicity, but I disagree about the validity of the structure created by players as the "sum of the parts" because it is more than just an interpretation it is the cultivation of a project by peer review and at least two layers of interactive developmental learning. They extend their existing into the existing of the "langue" or system that the project has become, insofar as it can be "made". Indeed it is, in my opinion, the existing of any individual making "using" synchronisation that provides the outcome of emotional rewards if indeed that is what provides the emotional rewards. Liking becomes the reward for functioning well in this “game”. There is also the notion of morphing from butterflies to bees, the irony of which is that the bee metaphor is ideological. We are not butterflies or bees but lepidopterists with caterpillars for brains. The reward alters according to the players as to numbers, specifications and so on. As we know we are “reduced” to herds or tribes of mammals in the large scale project, the “spectacle” of the situationists. Thus my thermeneutics includes the attitudes of individuals in the interpretive acts of processing for a “game” regarding their feelings about the processing, individually, on several levels, at various strengths, and at various speeds. I believe the posthumous Wittgenstein might approve of understanding it is the “game” that is existing whilst participants cultivate and maintain it as a game of getting it to and keeping it as a robust understanding [that is nevertheless fragile]. This also indicates that individuals can never achieve very large scale projects as robust, without wavering, because there will be too much variation in processing, speeds, strengths, and pluralities of it even within the one individual, and in fact in the chemical milieu as synchronicity.

A fairly easy link between the peer review, verbalisation and the pragmatisms of shifting towards the epicentre of the project can be noticed in a work by Latour [1947-]. A mixture of myth and observation was, and is, common in conversations everywhere, and can be read in the work of Rousseau [1712-1778] who noted that perhaps some peer review projects might clear up the actual knowledge about various people who are "out of range", not part of our quotidian conversations other than verbally. Tarde [1843-1904] however, pointed out it was possible to metricate behaviours so that measures of any synchronised behaviours could be taken. This is after all anthropological data so called where data is verbalisation, written accounts. Accordingly Latour refers to the theoretical application of phenomena made into data about monocultures, monocultural groups, as being both verso/recto. This is not as young students often say, reductive, so much as an eidetic shift towards project x, i.e. towards a project of any sort [but perhaps not the one they like themselves and thus the complaint]. Latour explains how the front of pages poured over by scholars, written on parchment, the verso, were given annotations on the back of each sheet, on the recto side. If we take this as an analogy of the verbalisation we begin to understand the impoverishment of this whole notion of measured data as "stealing" our eidetic shift. What is not apparent has to be added or imagined, verbalised, written on the back of the "narrative side" [verso] of the presentation. This is no longer a conversation but a "purified" presentation that becomes a written contract or covenant, binding flesh and blood to butterflies. By stealing I mean that our primary senses are our mammalian responses, the intimate one-on-one group to synchronicity, the mime conversations. Within one language these shift from conversations to communications over a few generations as Bickerton [1926-2018] describes in his work.

The actual monoculture is what actual people as pure layered and multiple processors with their own synergy as to synchronicity become as subservient to a/their "project" in which the individual participates willingly or unwillingly as their own feelings indicate to them how they feel about what appears to them in synchronicity as what is happening as best they can work it out. Clearly the fleshy, manual, will probably "win" over the verbal conversations, and pidgin speech is a robust understanding or no understanding at all.

How easy is it to be told the metanarrative? And then believe it so as to feel better about the consequences, taken on the shoulders of the eponymous "leader" of the flock. Some anthropologists recognise the problem by "living with" or living amongst monocultural groups in order to find out the "recto" appearances as much as they can. But of course unless the anthropologist alters their domicile, they are strangers, tourists,and as we might expect, there are instances where the "locals" carry out tricks upon anthropologists just as predators use camouflage to catch their prey, or actors to “fool” their audiences. We may note the constant corruption of any bright shining future, see Mason [1960-], depicted by butterflies, illuminated convenants, corrupted by flesh and blood dealing with synchronicity. In addition the data is collected from mammals already understood as a “flock” which we are not as human. My point is that this shows up the spectrum of relationships to synchronicity as I call it, the chemical milieu. The individual and the universe, to make it as eastern as possible perhaps, may be separated by geographical and monocultural epigenesis and developmental “controls” as we now know e.g. Carey [extant] and Edelman [1929-2014], yet joined together by our genetic commonalities.

Common synchronicity will go some way to the cultivation of a project of non-completion or the “art of living as an identity” whilst sharing common enough behaviours. In other words the conversations that can be had amongst a group of individuals who are self believing in a totality of one sort of human could, e.g. as eastern or western, black or white, indian or chinese, could it not, maintain a credible basis for all the specific peer review “projects” that emerge out of those conversations and those geographical and epigenetic circumstances all of which are linked to synchronicity, but in small groups, not a massive flock. The problem is then that conversations such as Said’s [1935-2003] orientalism and occidentalism just divides us rather than shows us how to comprehend our absolutely common humanity as individuals. Theologians find easy pickings amongst individuals who have had little exposure to the rigours of peer review, of shifting towards a project epicentre by tightening up the discourse and linking it to their mammalian "origins". The point of the teacher is to move towards the student so as to become students together as peers shifting to project x as varying opinionated centripetal groups yet aware of being able to shift centrifugally. The difference is not that theologians do not encourage rigour, it is that they do it using superstition. When we try that on children it must be terrifying for them.

Migration and Morphosis

In essay seven I discuss "**migration and morphosis**" as the way in which individuals seek to shift their here and now, that and how, to a tradition they like better than the one in which they feel they dislike or dislikes them. I explain why it is "normal" to experience an existential threat when this happens, yet it can pass.

-

So here in this essay I go out on a limb so to speak, and introduce a third sensory layer that has come to effect us all – the sensory layer of value transduced into actual coin that communicates as value but is in fact conversational, and also as flesh.

The way I shall do that in this essay is to use the term mammalian to relate to the "flocking" assessments of large numbers of us individuals. I think I will use individuals to refer to each of us since that is my belief, that we are all equally individuals. This also allows me to use the term "person" as the one or more of project “x” any individual may have in their eidetic shift towards x, and subsequent creations of boundaries to that shift. Thus the creation of a person becomes project x for any individual in which they themselves have sensory layers one, basic senses, and two, proper languages, Langue [seems to be langue singular and langue plural]. Thus in the eidetic shift within one langue and amongst conspecfics as to mammals, i.e. in our case humans, then there is a good chance of arriving at shared values eventually perhaps even on a large scale? Thus we see not only languages developing, and accents and so on, but we see all of those developing with cultures. So the culture could be understood as the mammalian phenomenon whereas the langauge is the more developmental basis of the secondary senses that deals with words and thus reading and texts and semantics, what goes where with what, the that and how of grammar and syntax; the butterfly world of words.

So far so good. But what happens when there is a tertiary sensory layer that allows values to be made fluid by altering the payment made to the mammalian individual who, as we are told over and over again by the cognitive science theologians, is basic to our being [whereas it is actually basic to our basic. Basic to our primary senses and thus to mammals as all mammalian senses of pain, joy, fear, hunger, and so on]. Thus the eidetic shift towards “person x” which is the work of an individual to “become x in their own way” is thus seduced not only by a second layer of processing, langue and the diachronous [which is not history but a dictionary, a semantic glossary of terms that **must** be used – believe me, attend any philosophy group in London and you will experience the emergence of **must** quite quickly once any meeting commences. All attempts at opening up conversations hit the **must** buffers early on in my now quite wide experiences of meetings amongst what are mostly neo-kantian neo-liberal i.e. paternalistic individuals, like it or not since they are educated by neo-kantian neo-liberals in the main, almost totally. Educated by shepherds in theological seminaries, hardly ever to leave their ivory towers to check the recto of their versos].

So the idea of shared authorship that for example Gadamer [1900-2002] was reaching out towards in his work, I believe, in my opinion, would require one individual to open a conversation with another individual and then jointly set up between them project x. This x would require an eidetic shift on both their parts. It may require a mammalian shift into discomfort, for the sake of the project. It may also require a conversational shift into a specific dictionary of terms, a glossary of terms that are of eidetic benefit to both. This then is the quintessential explanation of the shift into disciplines after Epicurus [341-270 BC] had alluded to, the “process out of which all appearances of the human condition emerge” right up to Erasmus [1466-1536], “the last individual to know everything”, as the model of the “philosophical king” or master of knowledge prior to the chaotic butterfly world of free speech [after the development of common language as uncommon, the right of “persons” of all sorts]. This common touch has had an enormous effect upon theological seminaries, has put it out on the street, homeless, so to speak.

So the shift from one individual knowing the that and how of pin making did not shift to the division of labour because of the badness of industrialisation as Ruskin [1819-1900] wrote and presumably felt and thought, but because we could. It had become possible to make more pins by sharing the dictionary and using the same semantic variables within the same grammar and syntax more or less within a limited dictionary, a text book we might say, an instruction manual. Bickerton [1926-2018] sort of supported this in his writing as to the importance of semantics in order to convert the possible three hundred thousand or so versions of a ten word sentence into the one sentence that actually made sense within a language. For semantics read dictionary as in synchronicity within this or any conversation in the butterfly world as the dictionary that holds sway over any shift towards communication, aka the occurance of identity as any extension of PMI and PMII as to everywhere and for all time, as if the person is trapped in a textbook like a lepidoterist seeking to pin down a flurry of mutating butterflies.

In addition to the possibility of programming using the language that pin making was, a shared eidetic that became specification writing and management of the uses of specification, the notion of one pin maker was quashed. The character of the pin making person was quashed. The notion of knowing everything had always been a lie, a conceit, a way of controlling the mammalian in us all as to the pushing towards speech and other actions, and pulling in of the correct words and sensed phenomena. Everything had always been this project x of despots and those not daring to be despots but dreaming of despotism/s. The way to achieve it however, is to cross that rubicon of the eidetic shift out of mammalian and into linguistic “territories” or rather one territory. Making that territory seem real was as we know from our developmental past out of mammalhood, the bread and butter of the wealth of nations. Thus english that went from england that gave its name to that promiscuous langue, to america that then built a huge war machine to keep its territory safe; not the last nation in the world but certainly the most aware of the need to beat mammals into submission rather than have them making their own eidetic shift to an alternative project x.

But what alternative?

What took over from language once the all knowing model, the Erasmus of cultures, was understood to be impossible? Actually the economist, the new dictionaries of the world language of fluidity of values, the selling of one's grandmother for a meal or a quick pleasure.

In more prurient terms, Simmel [1858-1918] and later Graeber [1961-], used the gold "chemical element" on the periodic table, a sort of metal that allows severance from the mammalian modes of psychic "pain and hurt" at a cost [valued in a dubious contest between its colour, that of the sun and yellow ochre, and its rarity in the conditions of being in general]. Handing over gold, in particular by using programs using the semantics of legal agreements that we call contracts of **settlement**. Thus ongoing battles over modes of eidetic shifts towards project x. Thus the projects of previous individuals, and thus the results of their eidetic shifts, and thus the robust fragile certainties of those boundaries of space as to "fiat economies" and time as their historical documents documenting the eidetic shifts they took, in the past, aiming for a future, along the same semantic "pathway". Although of course it was a pathway for mammals, for the flock, for the sheep following their shepherds, the statespersons, mainly men, who delivered "jerusalem" for the herds they were "accountable" to, who also fed them, and watered them, and kept them in "power" as all knowing and all seeing [thus remaining ignorant of the actual conditions under which they are existing "thinking recurrance" after the development of the very fiat economies they "support", yet by most accounts, even today, unaware of the nature of a fiat economy per se].

The trade off that seemingly in some ways knowingly took place is that in exchange for going off to war and dying for those one also fed and watered, the deal was to allow the "leaders" to do the eidetic processing that was required with other leaders so as to arrive at project x, "peace in our time". In doing so "they" came up with nuclear weapons or nuclear stalemate. In the periods prior to Erasmus the use of coin was also in place, part of the phenomenal milieu. But might could not always beat a settlement in gold, especially if verbal and without common support of the secondary sense. Thus primary sense fleshy rebellions, secondary rhetoric, tertiary gold, or war.

The trade off meant that apart from the need to maintain the fiat economy of the dollar, globally, by force of arms, as had been the pound, and as will be other super currencies, individuals were liberated from the need to die for their leaders. Henceforth we would be incarcerated, and less frequently killed, but only if we got in the way of the eidetic shifts the various managements were involved in when managing the projects of their scholars and peers, and in this they have been not only unhindered it seems to me, but also aided by those theological scientists who create, adimittedly partisan, dictionaries of words that make the use of coin, fluid value, permitted or indeed required. The partisan condition will clearly cause frictions, although the reasons for this is that the mammalian condition has not been clearly thought through relative to the linguistic and this new financial condition that we now exist in. These new phenomena have been created by us and have not been understood by us, that is my point. I am still working with these three senses, mammalian, linguistic, economic.

The seduction of the knower and the known, that I like of the work by Dewey [1859-1952] the pragmatist, easily becomes project me in project world, even project universe, in the simply mammal. Thus shepherd, thus flock, thus mass followings of all sorts, not just the traditional institutions but modern day gurus and nabobs all around the world. The important shift to our use of the secondary sense using language, integrated with our mammalian origins, went without much comment as far as I can find, and I have searched, and would indeed welcome news from others who are searching and have searched. The outcome of language should be, in my opinion, a big shift from the me who knows everything to the me who knows my existing is a robustly fragile certainty [understanding]. That I believe would have been fine. Open to conversations and eidetic shifting between Epicurus and Erasmus as a developmental period. Now developmentally explorative as to extending the secondary [which is not going well imho] and over reacting to the tertiary [because shiny beads overwhelm and outbid struggle almost always].

In a very partisan manner I will admit, I see the eidetic shift as I am calling it, in england, shifting towards a parliament in the early 19th century in which there was a small recognition of the need to shift to a position of extending the parliament into the economic conversations of “the people” metaphorically as to coin. We can see in Marx’s [1818-1883] Capital I, II and III, as explained by Engels [1820-1895], the thrust of an argument towards economics and away from literature. But there were at the time [and a wry smile to Lyotard [1924-1998] here because of his warning not to do what I am in the middle of doing, creating a narrative]. But this is a narrative of my theoretical position on the eidetic shift that I claim was made just after the french revolution that mainly introduced a new economic period of “post slavery”. See James’ [1901-1989] Black Jacobins for details and Horne’s [1949-] “The Counter Revolution of 1776” and then read Capital I, and note the slavery links. The european french revolution was of educated mammals standing against the horrors of enslavement. That "terror" as it turned out, the giving over to mammals what had been a literary spectacle for several centuries because of the middle ground of la france as to institutionalised and individual beliefs, humanisms.

The repugnance at the terror meant that the old shepherds of blood and soil, had very robust fragile understandings of eidetic shifting using mammalian wars and agricultural conditions, vassals, effectively slaves, simply transferred into factories. Those transferring the peasants into workers such as Stalin [1878-1953] also debunked the marxist error of the proletariat, as only having their bodies and the bodies of the fruits of their often intimate primary senses now romantically affiliated with their loved ones. The point was to open up dictionaries to conversations and thus for some the point became to close down conversations and force upon all one single dictionary, in that case the dialectical materialism of Lenin as understood by Stalin. These new workers, contemptuously called the new middle classes, as if we are born to mature as if in a class, wanted more and else and thus the communist manifesto was a hint at revolution and simply a replacement of leadership thus subject to the same, mammalian, issues of nepotism and corruption. For those doubting this see the literature available about this by for example Kolakowski

[1927-2009] and others listed in the references section of this book. Later revolutionaries such as Guevara [1928-1967] were readers as well as leaders, thus they were literary, well read. Labour party posters in the early 20th century spoke of bildung, self learning-and-teaching, but this seems to have slipped, far too rapidly, to tertiary senses of "wealth" by gold [and a "struggle to the death" proving that the rich and poor are linked by a common mammalian gene perhaps, rather than separated by spurious concepts of class other than in the various text books relating to each one; see for example Orwell's [1903-1950] Animal Farm].

Surely the whole point of the copernican revolution was to resolve the issue of subject-object. Thus the notion of classes of subject is repugnant to the whole point of "the enlightenment". The situationist movement so called was adamant about this shift from mammalian spectacle to the individuality of the individual and thus opening up conversations in the phenomenal milieu to all three senses; mammalian, linguistic, financial. Their critique was of the notion of culture as "big X" as some moral high ground. Thus for example the work of Home [1962-] provides a conversation on this although it is of little help, in my opinion, as to the understanding I am looking for in the eidetic shift. The angst is against authority and power but that is an incoherent mammalian angst of incandescent rage. The more erudite secondary sense of language must be used so that an individual can articulate themselves by bone and voice so to speak towards their project x, as individuals, and we can assume that in a democracy of any new sort the whole process must be this giant conversation in which individuals shift themselves this way and that. So rather than a shepherd and a flock of mammals, in which state of "flockness" we remain in any event but as a species, we talk our way towards and away from our projects and have the ability to fund all of it on the basis of our conversations and understandings. That is after all what Marx pointed out in Capital vol.I as to the "magic" of money as "flesh weighed without blood" [see for example Shakespeare's Merchant of Venice for an exegesis of this concept].

According to wiki the term erudite is used when instruction and reading followed by digestion and contemplation, have effaced all rudeness, that is to say smoothed away all raw, untrained incivility. In that sense civilisation is meant to be something like that described by the stoics, Cicero for example, where moral right is supreme. The values involved are of course measured by right thinking right acting individuals but that begs the question what right? The right of the incoherent flock is the basic right of all, not for example the one lone partisan text or pile of coins. The natural right, natures right, and so we are returned back to being mammals with shepherds as by for example Arendt [1906-1975] who was a student of Heidegger's and thus similarly interested in mammals rather than humans. Elias [1897-1990] who wrote “The History of Manners”, points to the way an eidetic shift with clear preferences for articulations, behaviours in public spaces augments the work of Goffman [1922-1982] who wrote “Behaviour in Public Places” without understanding this eidetic shift. Thus we have farmyard manuals rather than ways towards democracy and this is where we are with identity politics, farmyard textbooks on being the right sort of sheep. Hence my point here is that whereas Rorty [1931-2007] wrote “Philosophy and the Mirror of Nature”, and Lacan [1901-1981] on the mirror effect, they, in my opinion, misdirected readers to the mammalian question of a fragile certainty, and ignored the eidetic issues of the secondary senses of language and the tertiary sense of value per se as made fluid, and thus chemically perhaps strongly linked to the mammalian primary senses [which would help to understand why erudition is trumped by a fistful of cash, a handful of shiny beads. I did write about this, somewhat confusedly I do admit, in a research publication “for” architectural technicians. The article was called “The Morphological Construct” and the concept was pretty clear, the actual relationship to behaviour less so at that time. I urged technicians, and for that matter architects, to find out whether or not the “construct”, i.e. the totalitarian “project x” they were working for, with, whatever, was worth it! That still seems to me a good idea, although now of course I have a more erudite way of putting it! My notion is that the cash payment for working on a project is sometimes blackmail or salve to conscience because the project is not about issues that form part of any eidetic shift that is in train because individuals have shifted towards it at the mammalian level. Individuals are unable to achieve this other than in their faith in the flock and its literary sense and common sense about "gold" [see Weber [1864-1920] and Simmel [1858-1918]]..

But of course as some have stated, mostly it seems to me french students [professors], there was a counter revolution that was still based on those who were quite literally romantically inclined towards the quasi scientific work of Newton [1643-1727] that was on an eidetic quest towards a clockwork or mathematical "reality" [that could not be had]. I can write this because I share this view with Popper [1902-1994] who rather like myself had a habit of trying to please no-one and thus had few friends in academe or industry once his work had been made use of. Thus for a while Popper was held up as a paragon of freedom, and then as a disaster. This I can write because of an in my opinion worthy conversation about Kuhn [1922-1996] and Popper in a book by Fuller [1960-] in which Fuller shows how Kuhn reverts to a newtonian model of knowing whereas Popper holds fast to a developmental and robust frailty model. Of course Popper is known for inductive reasoning, but what is that compared with finding a way towards comprehending an eidetic shift in a phenomenal milieu that may produce "project democracy"? Predators and parasites flourish on ignorance. Knowledge is not however a cure but a product of processing relating to what matters, Bateson's [1904-1980] difference that makes a difference when it matters. The latter is often decided as a contest rather than as a meditation.

This then is the question. Can individuals such as we, all equal as mammalian beings, shift our eidetic clarifications through mammalian, seminal, requirements and thence through erudite articulations of the secondary sense, language, and in doing so avoid the filthy lucre in favour of decent lucre, the latter being essential to the economic fluidity of our mammalian existing as individuals, rather than as vassals in conditions of homage and allegiance to the project x of some other individual or group, especially if some tribe or leviathan, some culture, be it commercial or historic, or both, masquerading as Erasmus? It turns out that far from being the politics for the people, democracy is the politics of bildung, lifelong learning, for the many and also for the few. Learners and teachers learn and teach this fact about the way democracy for the flesh, the consubstantiation of "reality and spirituality", PMI+ with PMII+, so ++, both only existentially “real” tempt us into the condition of “knowing”everything worth knowing.

Social Pedagogies

In this final essay "**social pedagogies**" I discuss what seem to me better than older notions of social epistemology, and a lot better than older models of social engineering that use "empirical evidence" and "ethnic cleansing". This notion of social pedagogies is that what brings us to learning is the human condition itself as project-rich, [an alternative concept is "niche" rich, if only we can realise it]. We already deal with synergy individually, and the diversity of individual feelings is central to the feeling individuals have about settlement and survival. What I explain in these essays is that the settlement and survival is bonded to projects that overlap. Individuals can move between settlements because they are not so much virtual as chosen by choosing play or wisdom about projects, in effect.

-

I have been looking at the notion of bourgeois for some time now. It seems tainted for general use by the affection with which it is used as an insult against the rich as if nabobs are somehow "born" rather than "made", or as if Camelot [a time, place, or atmosphere of idyllic happiness] were A. True and B. Still the english speakers domicile of choice in a world in which every mammal has an enduring wish to be english in the literary sense which is of course risible yet indeed the only way to achieve it.

The petty bourgeois as a term of scorn against small merchant traders and artisans and a class neither peasant nor priveledged by grace and favour, as it appears in much of the socialist literature, seems a problematic term when reading Habermas [1929-] for example. He who has spent a lifetime trying to find a way to avoid mammalian or we could say Orwellian [1903-1950] disasters, having witnessed them at first hand.

It seems clear bourgeois is a problematic term. The etymology or development of the use of it for townsperson, bergers, so it seems, as well as more specifically used in literature obviously using the term in order to abuse rather than enlighten obscures the issue. Toulmin [1922- 2009] gives some indications of how the development of townsfolk, of a certain kind, might relate to classical upbringings of the greek antiquity sort of teachings. His comos and polis linked in cosmopolis as a metaphor of modernism. This translates into a mask for industrialisation and a "new order" stemming from the Jesuits in 1540, interested in education, research and cultural pursuits, thus actually pursuing the shepherd/flock model. This because the notion of a social world, as understanding the cosmos, the molar whole of existence, but as a polis of the priveledged of the greek city state. This was at that time the meeting of elites with families and slaves, their property, to shepherd, look after, care for. The updating to synchronicity may carry the concept of an elite with it, however the concept of synchronicity that I offer is one in which we are all equally mammalian. In that sense social life has changed since the great greek city state supposedly started its eidetic shift towards democracy. The move to Jesus was a first shift in the eidetic shift towards understanding the individual as the clarification of the human condition. This requires, however, a shift to sharing a phenomenal milieu between PMI and PMII, immersed in the chemical milieu of synchronicity. So not individual in society, nor humanity as "wholes", but a very different concept altogether, a deterministic mystery so to speak.

These days, after the enlightenment of the 18th century in Europe in particular, the individual has more importance in the scheme of things. So it would seem to me unhelpful if we consider as cosmopolitan the original notion of a cosmos and a polis of elites. What we need, however, is a secular pope, who monitors her mammalian flock and settles tertiary conversations about conditions on earth. Something that is within our grasp now we have extra terrestrial primary senses and synchronicity in our conversations thanks to wifi. In terms of a mechanical intelligence without the benefit of our organic PMII mysteries, then a potential regulator of global fiscal policies as a metronome year on year, for example.

As I have written in other essays in this book, all individuals are mammals first and foremost, our genes demand it of us. Thus as mammals all together on the earth we may consider it as our basic equality, something that could actually now be monitored and fed into conversations around the earth cheaply. These conversations, however, cannot at all be taken as communications, which is what they seem to be taken as at present. This links to our delusion about taking machine intelligence as artificial, which is risible. The spatial character of machine intelligence, as per PMI extentions, so PMI+ taken as mechanical because that is what they appear to be to us, must always "bow" to the organic intelligence of PMII+, the extension of PMII as neural intelligence since it is inextricably linked to PMI, to flesh, and the apparent mechanics of flesh and fleshy extensions.

There can be no spatial polis [a project considered in its ideal form for philosophical purposes]. Indeed were I to be, like any other, philosophical king it would be of my own project. In my opinion I would be perhaps unlucky if like Robinson Crusoe in the early days on my island all I had and could have was the island and my own company. The universe of phenomena that we mammals have developed in addition to those developed by any other mammalian specie is a universe of phenomena that I have found, in my own lifetime, to be of great interest and generally not disagreeable on the whole.

My notion, shared I think with Popper [1902-1994] as to the robust fragility of certainty, is for me an elegant way of reporting on my understanding of my own human condition. But I do not anymore have a project x of becoming a philosopher as I once did. At one point in my development I did believe philosophy might provide wisdom. And it does. But the wisdom provided is not erudite. Most of the time philosophical wisdom hurts other individuals, mammals like me who deserve mutual respect as do you as a mammal. Cultural wisdoms, tribal wisdoms, all seem to create harm rather than any sort of open milieu of phenomena within which we mammals may disport ourselves as we may or must according to synchronicity, the synchronicity being the "cause" of the fragility of our certainty, no matter how robust we might wish it to be, or think of it as. Schmitt [1888-1985] provides an exegesis of the harms resulting from sclerotic cultures. See also Cioran [1911-1995].

My polis, as I believe every mammals polis must be, especially when dreaming, is a romantic soliloquie and at root a solipsism. For me it is the basis of all research, a starting point that requires individuals to acknowledge how frail and uncertain it must be, this romantic knowledge of the universe and of me in it as a heroic figure as a baby, the place for unknowing heroism. Of course another mammal may have a gruesome knowledge of the universe and of themselves as some wretch. Such is the infinite potential of our mammalian abilities to dream as we develop into secondary and tertiary senses [not fully grown clones or copies of either of our parents]. The polis as niche.

Once I awake I argue that I commence my eidetic shift, or rather should do so in order to exist as free to consider any potential project as I may. My point is that each individual has possession of both flesh and imagination of their own in the form of the individual they are. To consider we own more than flesh and imagination is to consider that robinson crusoe owned his island. Such an eidetic shift is risible, and as you will know, this ownership was soon shared with another unexpected arrival in the phenomenon of Friday. Hertz [1881-1915] makes the same point about births, and also about deaths. The birth demands some sort of eidetic shift, as death ends it for one mammal and demands changes in the eidetic shifts of those that remain. The saving grace of mammals is their claws and legs and teeth and various instincts. But we have a secondary sense that is linguistic. Thus we can maintain instincts but in doing so seek to retain the mutual respect that a bunch of self respecting mammals might seek to have in having a language to converse with rather than mime alone. Mime can as we know help individual mammals to converse, but conversation using language offers a lot more. And here I must remind a reader that I say conversation not communication.

As Bickerton [1926-2018] points out we do however need to develop our uses of language. His was a linguists interest in it, but mine is that of what I would call a polymath, a student/teacher, a neoHumboltian [1767-1835]. One of us interested in learning rather than in wisdom, not being erasmus/erasmic, just learning so that my knowledge is capable of having more conversations with more other mammals who have learnt to be erudite with their own use of languge. If those other mammals are wise then that is not a problem unless they claim to be erasmus, in which case they are not any more wise in synchronicity. But to be in synchronicity it is necessary to understand it at least a little. Thus language claims made by mammals must not be on a take it or leave it basis. They must be conversational and then become eidetic shifts centrifugally into the beyond of conversations less relevant to any co authored project x. Or the conversations may become eidetic shifts centripetally into the focus of a project with no real centre, with no real boundary, and yet aiming for a system of ontics, entities about which facts and familiars are agreed upon as a robust yet frail certainty, between us as co authors. This requires as we intuit, an individual interpretation of phenomena, then a lexicon of entities, ontics, and thence a project x, understandings, that be spoken of and participated in using that ontic set, in peer review, in two polis'.

It really is difficult to note that the PMI and PMII conditions produce phenomena that appear as one milieu, the phenomenal milieu. These phonomena are then interpreted on the basis of the individual sensing we each have. As Fichte [1762-1814] and

Humbolt noted, after Kant [1724-1804], each individual can suffer and/or act by pushing and/or pulling on phenomena. The difference was pointed out by Fichte as a disposition to act, which became misunderstood as behaviour of PMI rather than as behaviour of the organism generally, and thus behaviour of both PMI and II. Comte [1798-1857] had noted a disposition to arrange as acting, particularly methodically, mechanically one might say. Thus an adoration of the mechanical arrangements that we are capable of, spurred on by the outstanding successes of Newtonian clockworks, has lead us to put life into mechanical intelligence, which is our current cul de sac. Comte's followers did even convert this adoration of the mechanical intelligence into a religion in the south of France I believe. Like some truly organic tribes that are known to have worshipped aeroplanes as gods. In truth it seems that the PMI and PMII links with their ++ allow us to link suffering to arranging and arranging to both PMI and PMII extensions such that we can have both conversations and communications that relieve our sufferings by arrangements of our own. Peers in the polis' express indifference rather than hubris, since each peer has its own polis.

Thus we would be mammals without masters, no shepherds, not part of any flock other than the grand flock of humans that at present covers much of the earth so it seems. Secular shepherds, secular flock, secular interpretations, mutual understandings [a balance to the predatory and parasitic symbiotic outcomes of our kind, that we know are both possible and problematic]. So the point now seems to be for me to point out how the tertiary sense of economics can be brought into a similar condition to where some few of us believe we are with languages. For a beginning it is clear that all those who earnestly believe still that language, or any other correlative system of entities, will allow us to know reality are not part of this new eidetic shifting that I claim we are capable of. The correlation such mammals seek is much more likely to be that of the plant, or language free mammal using tooth and claw to mangle their way through their hapless lives. None of them have managed to do more than be happy or sad in ways that we cannot truly understand because we cannot share an eidetic shift with them using language. We can only delude ourselves that they know us and we know them, a romantic gesture, a romantic soliliquie on pets and so on. If it were not romantic then we would be unable to kill mammals we know to be human, and since many of us are still doing this, then the reality is that we are able to be predatory and parasitic upon all mammals regardless of their actual genetic abilities to share eidetic shifts. Thus the rubicon that is language as to our condition separate from other genes, is not that of human but of the program those eidetic shifts have shifted us into. Langauge allows us to shift ourselves into conditions in which other humans are called inhuman, as both more and less human than human. And thus those less than human are "fair game" and only those more than human are to be given respect. It would seem to me that this state of affairs is risible, and that all human mammals should be considered equal. The problem is the project x having the wrong x usually demanding mammalian acts of dehumanising other human mammals. The notion of non human applied to human mammals should not be part of any eidetic shift. That is a lack of freedom on the one hand, and a stimulus to research on the other. From my own experience it seems as if the notion of the eidetic shift can only truly overcome the intuitive articulations of the mammals we all are by including the articulation of bones as well as of words and thoughts. Thus as we find migration, the need for wandering the earth, is part of what we need as a response to suffering, and/or to actions by PMI and/or PMII, to arrange organically and/or mechanically. The obvious diversity these alternatives allow mitigates against any sort of universal judgement globally other than the tertiary regulation of fiscal, renewable, annual, policies. The fluidity of the chemical milieu, the proliferation of the phenomenal milieu, the conversations and the inherent fluidity of mechanics to coin, as Marx explains in the early pages of Capital vol I, allows us to manage our sufferings using a fluid mechanics, if we will it.

And I must here note that if I go on with this grandeloquent typing I will turn into one of those philosophical types I wish to eschew. Thus I should leave any greater exegesis of the linguistic shifting to another volume if I have time. What I should do here is point out if I can, the ways that the fluidity of value has crept up on us and suspended the possibility of democracy by seizing it from the jaws of victory, as seemingly has been achieved by the faux-economists in our midst. The binary oppositions of positivist and socialist theologians claim their various mechanics of good and evil. In doing so they remove the chance for each and every individual to deal with their own suffering, to arrange things as they can or must for themselves, and then allow that in the fluidity of the totality as I have explained the totality is, indeed, fluid until we make it mechanical, and then again fluid.

By mistaking the tertiary conversation as an economical mechanics we produce a cage rather than a swimming pool. The aim must be to make the transitions from fluid to mechanical across the three levels of mammalian, linguistic and financial better understood. In commencing this task I refer to Bataille [1897-1962] and what he calls the accursed share. Remember this is conversational and so I do not invite Bataille lovers to swear that he did not mean this when he wrote his book. He may well have not meant this, but in my conversation I can and do here use it. It is a notion I can appropriate into an economic relationship such that the robust fragility of the confidence required in any economic venture demands an accursed share. This is exactly as Marx [1818-1883] described it in his voluminous works, especially capital vols I, II and III. However Kautsky [1854-1938] for example, called this share "surplus value" and elucidated his thoughts in Marx' Capital Vol IV, and that Luxemburg [1871-1919] also wrote of in her "Accumulation of Capital". "What is to be done" with any surplus? Thus, what is done with impure profit [that is to say not mutual profit] and its asymetrical accumulation and availability within project x ?

The solution Bataille gives us is to spend it on thankgiving. So the first point is to seek a profit through mutually participated in conversations and understandings [project x's]. The second is to use it in thanksgiving rather than putting it back into the tertiary realm. Bataille's example is Tibet. The thanksgiving is to be given to synchronicity as found. Thus research and learning but not projects in the tertiary. Rather the monitoring of symbiosis to ensure that mutuality at least balances the commensalist, predatory and parasitic outcomes that we are all too capable of in ignorance or pursuit of the wrong projects. This remember is a conversation and it is held with the work of a dead person, so do not blame him. In 2019 the concept of throwing money away is an eidetic shift many would I reckon refuse and instead make a reflexive shift in favour of clarifying thrift and parsimony over what they would also clarify as waste. I have been to a good many cattle markets around london, in which shepherds are trying to recruit sheep. One of the usual eidetic shifts is a reflex to the class war. The shift is often based on for example Gramsci [1891-1937[, who it seems made his shifts towards a project of Croce [1866-1952] whose discipline was like that of Vico [1668-1744], so that the concept of the diachronous was not a contemporary developmental dictionary and semantics but a past as real, as narrative, and as selectively narrative at that. This links also to Canguilhem [1904-1995] whose work on organisms and cells relating to the human condition I like. But his work as historian and colleague of Foucault [1926-1984] seems to have influenced the latter as to the use of history. Thus the relationship of Foucault to conversations about power are about the anthropological and behavioural as to games played rather than to the more common problem of interpretation of the eidetic shift. Consider as the three schools Frankfurt, Vienna and Berlin, where we find objective social and then individual, the last in Berlin as to education, the understanding of fluidity ruling over mechanics, that remains massively ignored compared to the other two, Positivism and Socialism.

One of the problems it seems to me that we are having is that large numbers of new people are developing attitudes to history objectively and socially rather than to dictionaries and conversations with other mammals, individually, other mammals who they dehumanise as much as those others dehumanise them by categorising them objectively and/or socially. The problem of this rhetorical use of the same language in order to create two systems of "power" is that the eidetic shift required sets off towards different projects. Yet both are project x for the mammals. The notion of the eidetic shift is that it is a conversational gambit not a war machine. So for example the example of Deleuze [1925-1995] where conflict is seen as an inevitable outcome of differing systems a la Schmitt rather than an inevitable outcome of individual shifts to different projects as permanently fluid. Is this more like Trotsky's [1879-1940] permanent revolution? No because it is class based and thus dehumanises as we can see in Mason's polemical rants. What are those projects differing on, but their systemic certainties? Thus they immediately fall prey to the delusion of the reality as real, or even as symbolic, as if the system is real.

That was the same Hegelian [1770-1831] problem of meaningfulness dealt with by for example Vattimo [1936-] in his work on Heidegger [1889-1976] and Nietzsche [1844-1900] advocating an "accomplished nihilism".along the lines it seems to me of the often seen on-line wifi buddhist existentialism suggesting a holding on and letting go, click on, click off, of meaning. I have even used that idea myself in the past as I struggled with my concept of a fluidity that became concrete. It is this sort of holding on to meaning that confused me about Heidegger's work until I read Jonas [1903-1993] who had studied under the same lutherian quasi jesuit theologian.

In his book on gnosticism Jonas asserts the pressure put on Heidegger to focus on pistis, faith, rather than knowledge. Thus I imagine there has to be something to have faith in, hence meaning as something to suffer and share that is satisfactorily mysterious since where does it come from? That certainly figures in Kierkegaard's [1813-1855] work and Existentialist writings most generally. This notion of some vitalist vital will to learn to suffer as explicity used in the domains of faith, belief, rather than as a search for knowledge that was still fairly commonplace in the 20th century as for example Tillich [1886-1965], the will to be as a faith in "meaning" in and of itself so that suffering, and the selling of remedies for suffering can continue unabated.

So the vitalist issue leaps onto the recto of the page and the only way to cope is to allow transubstantiation. And so back to the mammals being forced into primary relationships with entities rather than with phenomenal processing in order to vouch for their "faith" rather than mammals forced to make an eidetic shift towards expressions of their feelings using the secondary sensory systems that all humans have. The notion of fluidity from feelings of the chemical milieu as intuitions, eidetically shifting into secondary sense expressions, finding mechanical expressions and then conversations, moving from mime to descriptions and thus to clarifications of project x allows the possibility of co-authorship. Treating each other as equally mammalian, equally capable of eidetic shifts, equally capable of co-authoring leads to the tertiary sense of fluid values that is the very opposite it seems to me of holding on and letting go [who holds on, who lets go if not synchronicity itself?]. It is trading about the sort of eidetic shifts and projects that individuals might want to shift towards and/or away from. Thus a fluidity of feelings linked to a fluidity of values. This instead of a consubstantiation of goodness from say bread and wine that in consuming vouches for, becomes a token of, the piety of the consumer. If that sounds a bit like Weber's [1864-1920] epic work on capitalism then it is of course a fit that should be questioned for its fitness because it is the acceptance of vouchers as real in the "heady" rush towards x. In other words the social and the cultural is a product of individuals arranging and/or suffering together. The languages add restrictions to our innate freedoms hence the agonies of the mammalians struggling with fluidity denied by the mechanics of what is made allowable by communications and fiscal structures.

Is it not plausible that Saint Simon's [1760-1825] observations were obscured by the historical and progressive passions as the social sciences fought the positivist objections over which existing disciplines should have the upper hand for authority in this new enlightenment period? Physics seems to have wanted either pure maths or applied maths, and these diverged projects produced projects about systems and programming, with dialectical rhetoric using ontic, entities, objects, societies, cultures, suffering and arranging without making clear the projects that were the aims of various eidetic shifts. Indeed the consubstantiation of literature into piety is commonplace, Emerson [1803-1882] is a good example of that. The opposition between art and science is commonplace, when art becomes a social and linguistic [mechanical] product rather than individual expressions of the phenomenal out of chemical origins in synchronicity. The thanksgiving using money as the aim of the eidetic shift towards industrialisation rather than away from the mechanical and towards the chemical milieu which is closer to synchronicity as a god like embrace if we are allowed to become utterly romantic here [note the oftentimes close links between shamanic rites and the chemical embrace and subsequent enlightenment. Note also the often unlawful treatment of the "cul de sac" of depression using the liberating potential of chemical fluidity].

Any gradual accumulation of meaning we gain through existing, having experiences of existing, would seem commonplace in accounts of experience in general. According to scientists in the 20th century such as Baddeley [1934-] and Rose

[1938-] these accumulations of existing could be [wrongly] called memories. These can be experienced as appearing in the short and long term. This sometimes means immediate recall or the need to encourage recall in the various ways most of us seem able to achieve, some quicker and more accurately than others. [note that according to Fodor [1935-2017] none of us on earth knows precisely or at all how we manage to do this].

Some readers will be aware of the discipline of semiotics, the study of this isomorphism as to maps and legends and its use or interpretation. de Saussure [1857-1913] is one of several who describe the development of the isomorphism of schema over time as part parole or behaviour of individuals, and part langue, the appearance of an apparent whole system that allows the map, legend, tourism thing to work. De Saussure converted long term, we could say long term memory, and/or long term development, with notes [Simon [1916-2001] is the one I noted in my own work who made the point, a good one I believe, that had we not had the ability to write things down we would be in a perpetual quandry as to the totality of it all, adding it all up in the long term, diachronous, and having post it notes or synchronously, immediately to hand in the short or immediate term.

Now this ability to not only remember but also to write down and refer to something is common to both what is mapped and what is put onto a map and also to what is put into what some call long term memory. So for me there is ample room for confusion over exactly what matters as to what is happening with this concept of diachronous. I use imagined as the ability we have to have anything at all appear to us other than to articulate our skeletons, to walk to look so to speak. And I would imagine that any organism that had the capacity to do both, to articulate its memory, and its skeleton, would have an advangage as to building up a total language. [This is something I feel Bickerton leaves out of his own thesis on the development of language]. The totality of a language is in its dictionary [semantics] and its grammar and syntax the rules of which as we know are common in all human languages a la Chomsky [1928-]. Both Chomsky and Bickerton, however, leave out the developmental aspect of language growth whereby a studio group of elites enslave a worker group of mammals [and this is the difference between early and late human development as to early equals universalisation of individuals and late equals individualisation of existing]. In addition my own age tells me that whereas when younger I did more in order to arrange myself contrary to suffering totalitarianisms, it gets much more difficult to do, seemingly, in later life as to the value of alternative mechanics, many of which lay all around and about me as failed alternatives once imagined as viable, or probable alternatives but for a younger mammal.

The notion of synchronicity asks that we consider the dictionary as the diachronous so the synchronous makes more sense as the space of conversations between us in which we developmentally alter semantics and etymologies of entities, words. And we are not born with language. Bickerton reports that a child isolated without language loses the ability to learn a language at all. The developmental period is in the early years after the age of two. Prior to that no one knows, it may be of equal importance however only 70% of the brain has grown at birth, with the remaining 30% added up to two, after which the main wormy connections are hopefully in place head to tail in chains, the caterpillars I used in earlier essays. If language speakers are not around it seems that the secondary sense of language will not develop. Even more obvious is the tertiary sense of fluid value as I call it in which finance is used in order to cope with settlements as well as with wants and needs of any project.

Having deliberately attempted to keep each essay down to ten pages in this book I do not want to make this last essay over long, although I fear it already is for the unready. I want to not sum up but offer the theory and practice of a learning knower after the Berlin school. The situation of meaning is not and I believe never has been one of a loss of meaning totally. It is a loss of sense, of understanding, and this has always been of a project or two or many.

The massively parallel processing we do in the integrating synaptic galaxy; PMII. The layers of interactive cortex that provide intermediate and sublimal processing to what we have for ages considered as just in and out, sensory motor interactions with objects and other people. Even the notion of the difference between objects and other humans has denied what several are now suggesting is the human world that is ours alone as indeed Popper did. His indeterminacy is not of zero but of the fragility of the links between the phenomena that are unique to the human mammal that do not require behaviours but emerge as phenomena because of the processing we do and are already linked to feelings and developmental linkages to data transduced into objects including after early years a secondary sense of language and usually much later a tertiary sense of fluid values by way of coin, and now since the 17th century notes and in the 21st mere digits as tokens of value. I have to add that Popper was not, in my opinion, aware enough or at all of the ultimate fluidity of his indeterminacy in finance.

Furthermore, as Boltzman [1844-1906] and Durkheim [1858-1917] both made their eidetic moves, to clarify their soliliquie's as best they could, the contemporary speed of digital machines allows us to comprehend vast amounts of "data" as patterns we can use to see the ebb and flow of fluidity and interpret the patterns as projects of one sort or another. Individuals are somewhat unidentified in those patterns and yet they are included. The strange fact of contemporary living is as it ever was that no individual is an island for long or at all. The milieu of phenomena is however commonplace even if made different by the exact location in synchronicity as it emerges as a round earth upon which we are forced, by gravity and so on, and sometimes other mammals, to be existing upon and with. And in contemporary terms, it is a rare mammal that has all its own products and none produced by the bone or voice or pockets of another. None the less the mechanics of what is pulled and pushed by arrangement are ineluctably imposed upon the quintessentially fluid individiual existing in synchronicity. The extent of the removal of suffering is the extent to which suffering is removed from the individual, not the extent to which the mechanics communicates any removal, since the mechanics is quintessentially not fluid.

In my opinion it is this scare about a lack of certainty, a lack of meaningfulness, a lack of any mechanics, that produces the concept of panic amongst herds of mammals that are not human when things go dreadfully bad but mostly it is not panic but a shortage of time without the necessary period of development and adjustment to synchronous conditions as phenomena emerge from the fluidity into being as phenomena for us as humans. Soliloquising is one way of preparing for at least some alternative interpretations of any project, any understanding. Otherwise we must arrange the mechanics we have to hand, as Heidegger pointed out, with consequences often unanticipated and often the cause of yet more rather than less suffering. It seems then the removal of suffering is the aim and the impossibility of our ability to arrange by hand and brain.

The social pedagogy, what "brings us to learning" is our existing in synchronicity and to a great degree a willingness to have conversation rather than to have war. We need to have some common humanity about the projects we value and those we do not value, i.e. do not wish to shift to. The eidetic processing of making sense, of making patterns clear, may actually be better done now that we have satellites and computers to number crunch for us. Each individual however will have to come to terms with having conversations as a milieu between us all. Eidetic shifts to projects involve having ways in which we can enjoy individual eidetic shifts, as we do in our homes, alone or with our loved ones and they with us. We can also enjoy eidetic shifts towards institutional matters such as sports, transport, and educational buildings for example. And we can also enjoy eidetic shifts towards funding projects especially in a fiat economy. We can also prevent eidetic shifts where corporations seek to become leviathans and dominate our existing. This is, that is if we accept we are mammals all together with these additional senses of language and money. Current levels of emnity and fear mitigate against that. Current understndings in cross disciplinary conversations lead me to believe that those conversations mitigate towards this total understanding of the human condition as individuals developing eidetic shifts towards and away from projects those individuals like and dislike as we may.

The basis of any social pedagogy then as a learning mechanism is, as one might expect, the curriculum not just for childhood or early years or teenage years learning per se but is as bildung for lifelong learning where the theory and practice is this developmental relationship between individuals and their ability to shift eidetically and financially into projects and away from projects. The overall conversational milieu relates to mime and language and money as a three layered practice of developmental learning and co authoring projects in ways that individuals self manage their continuing developmental relationship to humanity as a whole, as mammals, and to the voices in the fiat economy as to their co authoring and refusing to co author the various projects. The important difference to current models of social pedagogy is that there can be no cultural model socially or globally or individually. Nor is there a maturing of youth into a fully formed adult member of any culture, be it of the entire mammalian population or of a smaller number of linguists and economists. The point of this is that the actual requirement for developmental learning will be instructed by the individuals themselves and synchronicity. Their developmental learning will allow them to co author, that being the only way to shift to their desired projects. The polis remains singular. What we find is the concept of there being constant and indeed prolific numbers of meaningful programs we can co author within synchronicity. First as conversations, then as peer review communications.

Thus projects, understandings, range from the very small to the large but not so large that we are pushed into being a herd or vassals to some master who is after all the same as us, or some missing master above synchronicity itself. The difficulty is that there is no certainty, however the theory behind this shift to synchronicity and its pedagogy of eidetic shifts as both theory and practice in one process, our own, is that we have never been certain of anything except that if certain then deluded. As the saying goes, we plan, synchronicity laughs. Or as Mallarmé [1842-1898] the existentialist poet wrote, almost, a throw of the die will never abolish uncertainty. In other words a cycle of theory and practice, an experiment in authoring alone or with others will always lead to a new experiment, because no matter how robust, all certainties are fragile, and always have been. The important difference is that the curricula will be that of each individual as one of many other individuals all of whom are equally human, and the thermeneut of their own projects for better or worse, for richer or poorer, and with a common mammalian egalitarianism shared by all.

The issue for synchronicity as a secular belief, is then a new symbiotic relationship between our species as mammals and our projects towards mechanisation as mammalian, linguistic and economic. Here we need secular popes, secular shepherds, and in place of mechanical text and dogma, the data and its conversion by “machine intelligence” into patterns that show the symbiotic relationships with planet earth as a whole species effect of symbiotic relationships to planet earth. Thus we have a whole new sort of global service to arrive at our individual understandings of synergy with our own eidetic shifts in fluid synchronicity. Thus we may learn the hardening of facts of symbiosis as one or more of predatory, parasitic, commensalist, competitive, mutualistic, and organic schema [in a state of flux perhaps] and have conversations about our mammalian behaviour at the global scale as a fluidity of conversations. Thus far we do not seem to have the appetite for such a project, but we do seem to have the understandings required to allow it. In the english speaking world and the yellow brick road world of the invisible hand that mechanises perfection [that as we find out is actually the hand of one of us hid from view] the mechanical has become god. Mathematics has become god.

Reason has become god. Whereas in truth fluid synchronicity is god and we commence in fluidity and eidetically shift towards and away from mechanisations in order to arrange ourselves against suffering, or temporarily towards settlement financially. It seems to me that by reducing suffering by arranging what we know we can arrange by hand and brain, we are able to mechanise the removal of suffering [predatory and parasitic schemas] far more ably than we can deliver happiness to all. In doing so we leave synchronicity fluid and available to all of us, as I believe it inevitably is, yet make alternative mechanisations irrelevant unless they can reduce suffering from “bad” schemata, and thus improve the common wealth of all. A fluid synchronicity and many understandings expressed, arranged by hands and brains in mechanical terms and thus ultimately doomed to obsolescence, the fluidity of our being being the only enduring as the organisms we actually are.

References

The works noted here are more thanks to the authors than references specific to the point at which the authors are noted in the text. Their works are relevant to the reader as conversations that can be had by a reader with those authors that as far as I am aware would not be seriously or at all contradicted by what I have written above, firstly as listed in essays and then as linked in general reading...

Contents

Thompson, Smile, Paperback ISBN: 9781784561192

Thompson, Voices, Paperback ISBN: 9781784563035

Thompson, Play, Paperback ISBN: 9781784564445

The Voice as Reason

Bickerton D, Language and Human Behaviour, University College Press, 1996

Heidegger M, Being and Time, Oxford, Blackwell, 1980

Jonas H, The Gnostic Religion, Beacon Press, 1958/2001

Nietzsche F W, Philosophy in the tragic age of the Greeks, Chicago, Regnery, 1962

Husserl E, [1913] Ideas, General Introduction to Pure Phenomenology, translation by W R Boyce Gibson, London, George Allen and Unwin Ltd, 1931

Gadamer H G, The Beginning of Knowledge, New York; London, Continuum, 2003

Hertz R, Death and the Right Hand, London, Cohen and West, 1960

Dreyfus H L, Being in the World, Cambridge Massachusetts and London England, MIT Press, 1997

Sartre J P, 1943, Being and Nothingness, London, Methuen & Co, 1981

Kaufmann W. Existentialism from Dostoevsky to Sartre, New American Library, New York + Scarborough Ontario, 1956 reprinted 1975

Derrida J, Of Spirit, Chicago, London, University of Chicago Press, 1987/98

Brentano F, 1874, Psychology from an Empirical Standpoint translated by Kraus O + McAlister L L, Routledge, N Y, 1973

History as Reason

Bickerton D, Language and Species, Uni of Chicago Press, Chicago, London, 1992

Comte A, Introduction to Positive Philosophy, Ferre F (ed), Hackett Publishing, 1988

Bateson G, Mind and Nature, Bantam New Age Books, Toronto, New York, London, 1979

Bloor D, Knowledge and Social Imagery, Second Edition, 1991, London, University of Chigago Press

Saussure F de, 1911, Course in General Linguistics, Duckworth, 1983

Fodor J, The Mind Doesn't Work That Way, MIT Press, 2000

Fodor J, Piatelli-Palmarini M, What Darwin Got Wrong, Profile Books, London, 2011

Feynman P, QED, Penguin Books, 1985/1990

Carey N, The Epigenetics Revolution, Icon books, 2012

Mitchell M, Complexity a Guided Tour, Oxford University Press, New York New York, 2011

Euclid, The Elements, Cambridge UP, (347BC) 1908

Vico G, (1744), The New Science of GiambattistaVico, Cornell University Press, 1994

Toulmin S, Cosmopolis, University of Chicago Press, 1992

Humbolt A, Cosmos, 1845

Fichte J G, Foundations of Transcendental Philosophy, Wissenschaftlehre, Cornell University Press, 1992

Marx, Grundrisse, Penguin Classics, 1973

Kolakowski L, Main Currents of Marxism, W W Norton + Co., New York, London, 1976, translated by Falla P S, 1978, 2005 version used

Kauffman S, Investigations, Oxford University Press, New York, 2000

Goldstein K, the Organism, American Book Company, New York Boston San Francisco, 1939

Brunswick E, 1947/1956, Perception and the Representative Design of Psychological Experiments, Berkeley California, University of California Press

Coherence

Husserl E, 1907 lectures, The Idea of Phenomenology translated by Alston W P and Nakhuikian G, MartinusNijhoff, 1964

Malthus TR, An Essay on the Principle of Population, London, 1798

Hegel G W, Philosophy of Right, Oxford University Press, 1967

Derrida J, Of Spirit, Chicago, London, University of Chicago Press, 1987/98

Machiavelli N, 1531, The Discourses, translated by Walker T J, London, Penguin Classics, 1998

Smith TV, Grene M, eds, Descartes to Locke, University of Chicago Press, 1967

Smith TV, Grene M, eds, Berkeley, Hume and Kant, University of Chicago Press, 1957

Kant I, Prolegomena to Any Future Metaphysics, Hackett Publishing, Indianapolis, 1983 – fourth publishing

Uexkull J Von, A Stroll Through the Worlds of Animals and Men, International Universities Press Inc. New York, 1957

Meillassoux C, After Finitude, Continuum, 2009

The Idea of the Eidetic

Morgan A ed, The Kantian Catastrophe? Bigg Books, Newcastle, 2017

Shannon CE, Weaver W, The Mathematical Theory of Commuication, University of Illinois Press, 1963

Habermas J, The Structural Transformation of the Public Sphere, Polity, 1992

Lewin K, A Dynamic Theory of Personality, 1935

May RR, A New Dimension in Psychiatry and Psychology 1960

Van Deurzen E, Everyday mysteries, Routledge, 1997

Yalom I, Existential psychotherapy, Basic Books, 1980

Damasio A R, Self Comes to Mind, Pantheon Books, New York, 2010

Greenfield S, The Human Brain, Phoenix, 2000

Wilde O, The Soul of Man Under Socialism, Penguin Classics 2001

Ponty M, The Visible and Invisible, Gallimard, 1964

LeDoux J, The Synaptic Self, Viking, New York, 2002

Pert CB, Molecules of Emotion, Pocket Books, London etc., 1999

Feynman op.cit.

https://www.jneurosci.org/content/37/30/7076 accessed 12/16/2019

Johnstone K, Impro, Methuen, 1981

Bickerton D, Language and Human Behaviour, University College Press, 1996

The Model of Social Utopia

Damasio A R, The Strange Order of Things, Vintage Books, New York, 2018

Greenfield S, The Private Life of the Brain, Penguin, 2000

Pert CB, Everything You Need to Know to Feel Good, Hay House, 2006

LeDoux J, 1996, The Emotional Brain, New York, Simon and Schuster

Bickerton D, Language and Species, Uni of Chicago Press, Chicago, London, 1992

Calvin W H, The River that Runs Uphill, The Sierra Club, 1986

Heidegger M, 1950, Hegel's Concept of Experience, Harper and Row, 1970

Descartes R, A Discourse on Method, London, Dent, 1978

Dreyfus H L, Husserl Intentionality and Cognitive Science, Bradford MIT Press, Cambridge + ;London, 1982

Uexkull J Von op.cit.

Husserl E, [1913] Ideas, General Introduction to Pure Phenomenology, translation by W R Boyce Gibson, London, George Allen and Unwin Ltd, 1931

Bhaskar R, Philosophy and the Idea of Freedom, Blackwell, 1991

Simon H A, The sciences of the artificial - 3rd ed ., Cambridge, Mass; London, MIT Press, 1996

McLuhan M, Understanding Media, New American Library, new York, Ontario, 1964

Arendt H, The Human Condition, Chicago, University of Chicago Press, 1969

Thompson, Play, Paperback ISBN: 9781784564445

Sunzi, The Art of War, -2500 UCT

Luhmann Niklas, Social Systems, Stanford University Press, 1995

Maturana H R + Varela F J, Autopoeisis + Cognition, D Reidel, Dordrecht + London, 1980

Bateson G, Steps to an Ecology of Mind, Paladin, 1973

Turner B S, The Body and Society, London, Sage, 1996

Bloor D op.cit.

Edelman G, Bright Air, Brilliant Fire, Penguin, 1994

Crary A M, Read R, The New Wittgenstein, Routledge, 2000

Post Positivism

Fichte JG, The Vocation of the Scholar, 1794

Comte A, op.cit.

Durkheim E, Pragmatism and Sociology, Cambridge UK New York USA, Cambridge University Press, 1983, translation by Whitehouse J C

Feynman R, op.cit.

Libet B, Mind Time, Harvard UP, 2004

Lyotard J F, The Post Modern Condition, Manchester, Manchester University Press, 1994

Engels F, The Housing Question, Coop Publishing Society of Foreign Workers in the USSR, Moscow, 1935

Mannheim K, 1936, Ideology and Utopia, London, Routledge, 1966

Smith TV, Grene M, eds, Berkeley, Hume and Kant, University of Chicago Press, 1957

Dewey J, The influence of Darwin on philosophy and other essays, 1997

Ayer A J, The Analytical Heritage: Russell and Moore, Harvard Uni Press, 1971

Bleicher J, Contemporary Hermeneutics, London and new York, Routledge and Kegan Paul, 1980

Gadamer H G, The Beginning of Knowledge, New York; London, Continuum, 2003

Latour B, We Have Never Been Modern, Harvester/Wheatsheaf, 1991;1993

Rousseau JJ, Discourse on Inequality, Oxford World Classics, 1999

Tarde G, Social Laws, An Outline of Sociology, 1899

Latour B, Lepinay V A, The Science of Passionate Interests, Prickly Paradigm Press, Chicago, 2009

Bickerton D, op.cit.

Mason P, Clear Bright Future, Allen Lane, 2019

Carey N, op.cit.

Edelman G, The Remembered Present, Basic Books, New York, 1989

Said E, [1978] Orientalism, Penguin Books, London, etc, 1991

Migration and Morphosis

Ruskin J, Unto This Last, 1860, Filiquarian Publishing, LLC, 2007

Simmel G, the Philosophy of Money, London and New York, Routledge, 2004

Graeber D, Debt, Melvillehouse, 2012Dewey

Marx K, Capital Vol.1, Penguin Classics, 1990Lyotard

CLR James, The Black Jacobins,

Horne G, The Counter Revolution of 1776, New York Uni Press, 2014

Stalin J, Leninism Vol II, Modern Books Ltd, 1933

Home S, The Assault on Culture, London, AK Press, 1988

Kolakowski L, Positivist Philosophy, Pelican Books, Uk, Australia, 1972Orwell

Arendt H, The Human Condition, Chicago, University of Chicago Press, 1969

Elias N, The History of Manners, Pantheon Books, NY, 1978

Goffman E, Presentation of the Self in Everyday Life, Doubleday Anchor, 1959

Rorty R, Philosophy and the Mirror of Nature, Oxford, Blackwell, 1980

Lacan J, Ecrits A Selection, London, Tavistock, 1977

Weber M, The Protestant Ethic and the Spirit of Capitalism, London, Routledge, 2001

Simmel G, the Philosophy of Money, London and New York, Routledge, 2004

Newton I, Mathematical Principles of Natural Philosophy, 1687/1728

Popper K, Conjectures and Refutations, London, Routledge, 1965

Plotkin H, The Nature of Knowledge, Allen Lane, 1994

Fuller S, Kuhn vs Popper, Icon Books, 2003

Bateson G, Mind and Nature, Bantam New Age Books, Toronto, New York, London, 1979

Social Pedagogies

Habermas J, The Structural Transformation of the Public Sphere, Polity, 1992

Orwell G, Animal Farm, 1945

Toulmin S et al, The Architecture of Matter, Hutchinson, 1966

Popper K, The Open Universe, Routledge, 1995

Schmitt C, Concept of the Political, Uni of Chicago Press, Chicago and London, 1996

Cioran EM, A Short History of Decay, Penguin Books, 2018

Hertz R, Death and the Right Hand, London, Cohen and West, 1960

Bataille G, The Accursed Share, Zone Books, 1993 [1949]

Kautsky K, Karl Marx, Theories of Surplus Value, Lawrence and Wishart, London, 1951, Capital, Vol.IV

Luxemburg R, The Accumulation of Capital; Edited by Dr. W. Stark, London, Routledge and Kegan Paul Ltd; 1951

Canguilhem G, 1966, The Normal and the Pathological, Zone Books, New York, 1989

Foucault M, The Birth of Biopolitics, New York, Palgrave, 2004

Gadamer H G, The Beginning of Knowledge, New York; London, Continuum, 2003

Bickerton.op.cit

Deleuze G, Guattari F, Thousand Plateaus, University of Minnesota Press, 1987

Trotsky L, The Permanent Revolution, Socialist Resistance, London. 2007

Vattimo G, 1985/1988, The End of Modernity, Cambridge, Polity Press

Kierkegaard see Kaufmann W op.cit

Tillich P, The Courage to Be, Yale, 1952/2000

Weber M, The Protestant Ethic and the Spirit of Capitalism, London, Routledge, 2001

Emerson R W, Introducing the Mystic Swedenborg, Ed.McNeilly S, The Swedenborg Society, London, 2009

Baddeley A D, Your Memory, Sidgwick and Jackson, 1982

Rose S, 1993, The making of memory, Bantam Books, London

Fodor J, The Mind Doesn't Work That Way, MIT Press, 2000

Simon H A, The sciences of the artificial - 3rd ed ., Cambridge, Mass; London, MIT Press, 1996

Chomsky N, Syntactic Structures, Mouton, The Hague, 1957

Popper op.cit.

Durkheim E, Elementary Forms of Religious Life, Tr.by J Ward Swain, George Allen and Unwin Ltd, 1915

Mallarme S, Un Coup de Des jamais n'abolira le Hasard, Wave Books, 2016

Thompson W, Wander, Self Published, 2020

Glossary of terms in aid of Eidetic Shifting:

Cosmogony: the study of the origin of being.

Eidetic shift: the ability to clarify the outcomes of cycles of processing so that interactions between conspecifics become understandings and vice versa by way of an ultimate beginning in the chemical milieu and ending in mechanical intelligences of one sort or another.

Project x: any focus of any eidetic shift that can be understood "mechanically" by one or many conspecifics, where x is merely the epicentre of that mechanical understanding.

Understanding: the result of an eidetic shift to x such that the project seems to have a context [boundary] relative to its epicentre by our ability to tranduce the chemical milieu by way of phenomena into the three mechanisations of flesh, languages and value.

Phenomenon: the result of the processing by conspecifics immersed in synchronicity thus experiencing a phenomenal milieu, a phenomenal existing.

Synchronicity: the universe as god thus unknowable but appearing to us as phenomena yet in fact fluid, a chemical milieu.

PMI: protein mass I, the flesh and extensions of it that appear as materiality as knowing becomes knowledge and dogma.

PMII: protein mass II, the neural synaptic galaxy or rather its phenomenal productions and thus the introduction of mysteries in addition to the chemical mysteries of synchronicity itself that also, of course, effects both PMI and PMII. Note this concept is intimate with dynamic homeostasis and experiencing because linked through flesh to processing and the chemical milieu and the production of phenomena that appear to us individually.

Butterflies: I use this term for empty signifiers that are phenomena in knowing that become known and aquire specific relationships in any flutter [group of butterflies] by way of eidetic and social shifting.

Limbo: a welcome alternative to the term nihilism. Vattimo [1936-] uses this term, but much as I like his work, the term seems to upset flesh and I believe this is sometimes because as with Moore [1873-1958] examples of existing as flesh can usually be given quite easily thus refuting nothingness. Limbo seems harder to refute and gives us an existential conversational beginning to sharing the management of understanding without that risible refutation of nihilism having so much purchase in such conversations.

Existential spread: the phenomenal content of the existential framing aplied by an individual centripetally to the phenomenal milieu appearing thus core beliefs and core contexts for understanding can be managed.

Accomplished existentialism: a shift away from Vattimo's [1936-] nihilism by using triage and thermeneutics in order to overcome the problem with hermeneutics [that I acknowledge along with Vattimo and Gadamer [1900-2002] as an issue of great importance] in that the flesh produces the phenomenal milieu as a "humanism". I believe this helps solve the difficulties encountered by such as Rorty [1931-2007] and Habermas [1929-] [who are otherwise hoisted on the petard of socialisms]. This poses issues about the phenomenal and eidetic milieu that remains work in progress in 2020. The term butterfly seems to be "known phenomena" socialised as per Searle's [1932-] concept of "truth statements" extended to valid and/or validated opinions.

The author started writing as a child. By seven wanted to be an architect. By twenty four had become a builder. By thirty four had become an architect registered and working in the uk.

At the age of fifty he decided that architecture as a discipline was a social science of some sort. On this basis he earned a masters at UCL and then a phd at Heriot Watt for discovering and defending a philosophical position based on interpretation he now calls thermeneutics.

When teaching about cultural contexts at the university of ulster architectural school [2001 - 2010], the link between perception and emotion became central to his interest. At which point he retired to write about understanding, in a series of books, this one being the fourth.

The first three were about sharing the management of understanding. This fourth is different in that rather than theology, he offers eidetic shifting as an understanding of the way to abide as one species on the shared earth with an emotional investment in each other's well being, an investment bank like no other...

Art by Georgina Trevor

9781784566876
SD - #0051 - 060826 - C0 - 210/148/8 - PB - 9781784566876 - Matt Lamination